THE CRIME MOVIE AND TV LOVER'S GUIDE TO
LONDON

THE CRIME MOVIE AND TV LOVER'S GUIDE TO
LONDON

CHARLOTTE BOOTH
&
BRIAN BILLINGTON

WHITE OWL
AN IMPRINT OF PEN & SWORD BOOKS LTD.
YORKSHIRE – PHILADELPHIA

First published in Great Britain in 2024 by
White Owl
An imprint of
Pen & Sword Books Ltd.
Yorkshire - Philadelphia

Copyright © Charlotte Booth and Brian Billington, 2024

ISBN 978 1 39903 130 1

The right of Charlotte Booth and Brian Billington to be identified as authors of this work has been asserted by them in accordance with the Copyright, Designs and Patents Act 1988.

A CIP catalogue record for this book is available from the British Library.

All rights reserved. No part of this book may be reproduced or transmitted in any form or by any means, electronic or mechanical including photocopying, recording or by any information storage and retrieval system, without permission from the Publisher in writing.

Printed and bound in India by Replika Press Pvt. Ltd.
Design: SJmagic DESIGN SERVICES, India.

Pen & Sword Books Ltd. incorporates the imprints of Pen & Sword Books: After the Battle, Archaeology, Atlas, Aviation, Battleground, Discovery, Family History, History, Maritime, Military, Politics, Select, Transport, True Crime, Fiction, Frontline Books, Leo Cooper, Praetorian Press, Seaforth Publishing, Wharncliffe and White Owl.

For a complete list of Pen & Sword titles please contact

PEN & SWORD BOOKS LIMITED
George House, Units 12 & 13, Beevor Street, Off Pontefract Road, Barnsley, South Yorkshire, S71 1HN, England
E-mail: enquiries@pen-and-sword.co.uk
Website: www.pen-and-sword.co.uk

or

PEN AND SWORD BOOKS
1950 Lawrence Rd, Havertown, PA 19083, USA
E-mail: uspen-and-sword@casematepublishers.com
Website: www.penandswordbooks.com

CONTENTS

ILLUSTRATIONS 7

INTRODUCTION 11

CHAPTER 1
GANG CRIME 14

CHAPTER 2
ROBBERIES 40

CHAPTER 3
MURDER 64

CHAPTER 4
SERIAL KILLERS 70

CHAPTER 5
ESPIONAGE 75

CHAPTER 6
TERRORISM 112

CHAPTER 7
MISCELLANEOUS CRIMES 119

CHAPTER 8
TV DRAMAS 134

CHAPTER 9
RELATED SITES 167

CHAPTER 10
PUB CRAWL 169

CHAPTER 11
CHURCH TOUR 182

CHAPTER 12
CEMETERY TOUR 187

CHAPTER 13
PICTURE AND PLAYHOUSES TOUR 189

INDEX 194

ILLUSTRATIONS

All photographs are by the authors unless stated otherwise.

1. 37-38 Hatton Garden, EC1N 8EB
2. St John's Gate, 26 St John's Lane, EC1M 4BU
3. 16 Whittlesey Street, Lambeth, SE1 8SZ
4. 2 Theed Street, SE1 8ST
5. 38-42 St John Street, Smithfield, EC1M 4DL
6. Blackman's Shoes, Cheshire Street, Shoreditch, E2 6EH
7. 13 Park Street, Borough, SE1 9AB
8. Botts Mews, W2 5AG
9. 18 Pottery Lane, W11 4LZ
10. 98 Holland Park Avenue, W11 3RB
11. 27 Bartholomew Street, SE1 4AL
12. Spit and Sawdust, 21 Bartholomew Street, SE1 4AL
13. Repton Boxing Club, Cheshire Street, Shoreditch, E2 6EG
14. 88-90 Hatton Garden, EC1N 8PN
15. 371 Mount Pleasant, WC1X 0BD
16. Hat & Mitre Court, EC1M 4EF
17. Café de Paris, 3-4 Coventry Street, W1D 6BL
18. Paddington Station, Praed Street, W2 1HB
19. Cavita, 56-60 Wigmore Street, W1U 2RZ
20. Savoy, Strand, WC2R 0EZ
21. Burlington Arcade, 51 Piccadilly, W1J 0QJ
22. Sarum Chase, 23 West Heath Road, Hampstead, NW3 7UU
23. Hampstead High Street Police Station, 26 Rosslyn Hill, NW3 1PA.
24. St Pancras, Euston Road, N1C 4QP (courtesy of Colin on Wikimedia Commons)
25. Smithfield Market, Grand Avenue, EC1A 9PS
26. Wandsworth Prison, Heathfield Road, SW18 3HU (courtesy of geography.org.uk from Wikimedia Commons)
27. Northumberland House, Lower Square, Isleworth, TW7 6RL
28. North Street, Isleworth, TW7 6RE
29. 4 Swan Street, Isleworth, TW7 6XA
30. Liverpool Street Station, Liverpool Street, EC2M 1QT
31. Ely Court, Hatton Garden, EC1N 6RY
32. Trafalgar Square, WC2N 5DN (courtesy of Charlie Forman, Wikimedia Commons)
33. Whitely Asset Management Ltd, 116 Princedale Road, W11 4NH
34. Aldwych Station, Surrey Street, WC2R 2ND (courtesy of Chris Roberts, Wikimedia Commons)
35. 8 Endsleigh Gardens, WC1H 0EG
36. Paddington Platform One, Paddington Station, Praed Street, W2 1HB

37. 18 Denbigh Close, W11 2QH
38. Jubilee Gardens, Belvedere Road, SE1 7PG
39. UCL, Malet Place, WC1E 6AE (courtesy of Paul Brockenhurst)
40. Westminster Abbey, Broad Sanctuary, 20 Deans Yard, SW1P 3PA
41. HMP Wormwood Scrubs, 160 Du Cane Road, W12 0AN
42. Old Bailey, EC4M 7EH (courtesy of GrindtXX on Wikimedia Commons)
43. Paddington Station Taxi Rank, Praed Street, W2 1HB
44. Regent Square Gardens, WC1H 8HZ
45. Senate House University of London, Malet Street, WC1E 7HU
46. Victoria House, 37-63 Bloomsbury Square, WC1B 4DA
47. Sotheby's, 34-35 New Bond Street, W1A 2RP
48. Malaysia House, 57 Trafalgar Square, WC2N 5DU
49. Westminster Bridge Road, SE1 7GA
50. Somerset House, Strand, WC2R 1LA (courtesy of Emperorzurg123, Wikimedia Commons)
51. The Reform Club, 104 Pall Mall, SW1Y 5EW (courtesy of philafrenzy, Wikimedia Commons)
52. Barbican Centre, Upper Frobisher Crescent, Silk Street, EC2Y 8HD
53. 1 Stanley Gardens, Notting Hill, W11 2ND
54. Rules Restaurant, 34-35 Maiden Lane, Covent Garden, WC2E 7LB
55. 7 Spring Gardens, SW1 2BU
56. Sonic Digital, 71 Praed Street, Tyburnia, W2 1NS
57. Fan Bridge, Paddington Basin, North Wharf Road, W2 1LF
58. Brewdog, Harbet Road, W2 1AJ
59. Fantasia Grill House, 28 Praed Street, W2 1NH
60. Leadenhall Market, Gracechurch Street, EC3V 1LT
61. 3A/B Belvedere Road, SE1 7GP
62. Buckingham Palace, SW1 1AA (courtesy of Diego Delso, Wikimedia Commons)
63. Holborn Police Station, 15 Lamb's Conduit Street, WC1N 3NR
64. Marble Arch, W2 2UH
65. The Farmiloe Building, 34-36 St John Street, EC1 4AZ
66. Tower of London, EC3N 4AB
67. Elm Court, Middle Temple, EC4Y 7AH
68. James Smith & Sons, Hazelwood House, 53 New Oxford Street, WC1A 1BL
69. National Theatre, Upper Ground, SE1 9PX
70. 18 Lloyd Square, Islington, WC1X 9AJ
71. Bank Tube, Cornhill, EC3V 3LR
72. Borough Market, Southwark Street, SE1 1TL
73. Lilian Knowles House, Sanctuary Students, 47-50 Crispin Street, E1 6HQ
74. Farringdon Tube Station, Cowcross Street, EC1M 6BY
75. St Martin's Lane Hotel, 45 St Martin's Lane, WC2N 4HX

76. College of Arms, 130 Queen Victoria Street, EC4V 4BT (courtesy of philafrenzy on Wikimedia Commons)
77. Old Royal Naval College, Greenwich, King William Walk, SE10 9NN
78. 15 Palace Court, W2 4LP
79. Piccadilly Circus, W1V 9LB
80. Millwall Football Ground, Senegal Road, SE16 3LP
81. Surrey Quays Tube, Rotherhithe Old Road Entrance, SE16 2PP
82. 122 Oldfield Grove Road, SE16 2NE
83. Footbridge, Oldfield Grove Road, SE16 2NE
84. 55 Silwood Street, SE16 2AW
85. 6A Woburn Walk, WC1H 0JL
86. Curzon Bloomsbury, The Brunswick Centre, WC1N 1AW
87. Guy's Hospital, SE1 9GU
88. Tate Modern, Bankside, SE1 9TG
89. Barbican Crescent, Silk Street, EC2Y 8HD
90. Russell Square, WC1B 4JA
91. Tower Bridge, Tower Bridge Road, SE1 2UP
92. Averard Hotel, 16 Lancaster Gate, W2 3LH
93. The Observatory, 64 Marchmont Street, WC1N 1AB
94. Greenland Dock, Swedish Quay, SE16 7UF
95. Greenland Surrey Quays Pier, SE16 7TY
96. Westfield London, Ariel Way, W12 7GF
97. Florin Court, 6-9 Charterhouse Square, Barbican, EC1M 6EU
98. Charterhouse Mews, EC1M 6AH
99. The Charterhouse, Charterhouse Square, EC1M 6AM
100. 4 New Square, WC2A 3RJ
101. New Scotland Yard, Victoria Embankment, SW1A 2JL
102. Fabric Nightclub, 77A Charterhouse Street, EC1M 6HJ
103. The Bargehouse, Oxo Tower Wharf, Barge House Street, SE1 9PH
104. The Bargehouse, Oxo Tower Wharf, Barge House Street, SE1 9PH (door 16)
105. Sherlock Holmes Statue, Baker Street Underground Station, Marylebone Road, NW1 5LJ
106. Sherlock Holmes Museum, 221b Baker Street, NW1 6XE
107. Globe Tavern, 8 Bedale Street, Borough Market, SE1 9AL
108. The Ship & Whale, 2 Gulliver Street, SE16 7LT
109. Ten Bells Pub, 84 Commercial Street, E1 6QQ
110. Ye Olde Mitre Tavern, 1 Ely Court, EC1N 6SJ
111. The Toucan, 19 Carlisle Street, W1D 3BY
112. The Blue Posts, Berwick Street, W1F 0QA
113. Scarfes Bar, Rosewood Hotel, 252 High Holborn, WC1V 7EN
114. George-in-the-East Crypt West, 14 Cannon Street Road, E1 0BH
115. St Lawrence Jewry C of E Church, Guildhall Yard, EC2V 5AA (courtesy of Diego Delso, Wikimedia Commons)

116. American International Church, 79a Tottenham Court Road, W1T 4TD
117. Isleworth Cemetery, Park Road, Isleworth, TW7 6AZ
118. Royal Albert Hall, Kensington Gore, South Kensington, SW7 2AP (courtesy of Reinhold Möller, Wikimedia Commons)
119. Empire Cinemas, 63-65 Haymarket, SW1Y 4RL
120. Criterion Theatre, 218-223 Piccadilly, W1J 9HR
121. Richmond Theatre, 1 Little Green, Richmond, TW9 1QH

INTRODUCTION

What you are holding in your hand is the third guidebook we have written about London which have followed an interesting curve. We started with the *Movie Lover's Guide*, then the *True Crime Lover's Guide* which then morphed to create the *Crime Movie Lover's Guide*. Each one has taken us on an interesting journey through London and through movies and the public's relationship with them. The crime movie genre is one that has fascinated movie lovers of all ages since silent movies made their debut. In the 1930s in the US crime movies were the most popular genre after romance and this has remained a constant since.

What is a crime movie?

Crime movies have developed over the years but essentially, they all have crime at the centre of the plot, although this can of course be presented from many different angles. Between the 1930s and the 1980s more than 26% of British film production was in the crime genre, and by the end of the millennium this had increased to nearly 50%.

So, crime is clearly big business but unlike many genres these films do not follow a straightforward plot trajectory due to the numerous sub-genres which include cosy murder (*Poirot*), gangster (*Lock Stock and Two Smoking Barrels*), film noir, courtroom dramas (*12 Angry Men*), prison (*Scum*), serial killers (*American Psycho*), psychos (*Psycho*), police led (*Luther*), espionage (*James Bond*), murder mystery (*Jonathan Creek*) and terrorism (*Profile*).

Within each of these sub-genres the hero can be the villain, with the police trying to catch them, or the victims depending on where the audience sympathies are meant to lie. This change in perspective can make for interesting viewing. Take *Lock Stock and Two Smoking Barrels* for example, where there are no 'good guys' per se – just different groups of criminals all with the same aim, although it is made clear who the 'good, bad guys' are. Add to that a franchise like *Luther*, where as a cop John Luther is probably the 'good guy' but has some pretty unorthodox ways of working and seems to be on the verge of being suspended at all times, showing he is a 'bad, good guy'. These subversions of the sub-genre make the crime genre in general varied and fascinating.

Additionally, when filmed from the perspective of the villain it does show that life isn't as straightforward as 'good guys' and 'bad guys' as we are introduced to their personalities, hardships and motivations. When Idris Elba was asked about his character Stringer in *The Wire* he said he was based 'on dudes that I knew when I was growing up in Hackney. They weren't gangsters, they were the nicest fellas in the world,' showing that whilst they may engage in criminal activities, they were just normal people living their lives. And that could be part of the attraction.

Why is crime so popular?

But why do we love crime films so much? There are many reasons crime as a genre is so popular. One reason is that it reassures the audience that good will always triumph over evil and that justice will ultimately prevail.

Another reason is that it is a glimpse into a world which for the vast majority of the audience have no experience, or it can be a social commentary on how bad decisions, lack of opportunities or bad luck can spiral into a life of crime (*Inside Man*).

The crime genre often provides an insight into a world which is real enough, and recognisable enough to be believable but from a safe distance providing much needed escapism. It also provides the opportunity to watch people (fictional) suffer and Pierce Brosnan stated: 'People just love seeing other people in jeopardy ... it is the same fascination as driving by road accidents. You swear you are not going to be one of those people who look, but you look anyway.' It shines a mirror on society and the mayhem of the criminal underworld, following underdog characters who refuse to play by the rules, as well as a justice system that doesn't always have the best motivations at heart.

A new addition to the crime movie genre is the absurdist capers which have dry humour at their core and has become a staple for many British movies (*Lock Stock and Two Smoking Barrels, The Gentleman, Snatch*) which on one hand are brutal and violent and yet on the other hand are also ridiculously absurd, essentially providing entertainment and escapism for the audience, whilst poking fun at the genre at the same time.

However, for many the attraction is the interactive nature of a good crime film that draws the audience in – the act of trying to work out whodunnit and why before the reveal at the end.

How to use this book

What you have in your hands is a guidebook of the nearly 650 locations used in 76 movies and 12 crime TV dramas. Of course, this is not a definitive guide to all crime movies ever made in London. It's a snapshot, or trailer, of some of the filming that has happened in this wonderful city.

One of the challenges with a book of this kind, is that due to the nature of the films often scenes are filmed in run-down areas of London or areas which are due to be renovated which leads to many locations no longer being recognisable. Add the challenge of many films being created within a studio environment meaning they were not filmed on location at all. Another challenge included London-based movies being filmed in Birmingham or Cardiff rather than the capital. This has meant that there are some films like *Sweeney Todd: The Demon Barber of Fleet Street* (2007) or TV shows like *You Don't Know Me* (2021), which have not been included as there are no London locations to show.

However, the locations we have identified are laid out in various ways to make your journey around London easier. The films are initially in alphabetical order according to genre (gangster, robbery, murder, serial killers, espionage, terrorism, miscellaneous and TV dramas) with all the locations from that film laid out according to plot rather than area.

Then there are several tours according to special interest which include a church and cemetery tour, a picture house and theatre tour and of course the pub crawl although we absolutely do not recommend trying to complete this in one day. One of the most important aspects of the book for creating your own bespoke tours will be the indices which are laid out according to film title, TV show, location and area of London, meaning you will be able to create a bespoke tour based on your location in London at any particular time.

You will notice that there are no maps in this book, which is a considered choice as the 650 location sites cover the whole of London, from Richmond to Rotherhithe and would require pages and pages of maps to be effective – the A-Z does this better than we can so instead we have used postcodes which can be put into your map app on your smart phone and will take you to the specific location. If the postcode is 'close' to but not the exact location, then details in the entry will guide you to the location. This book is designed to be interactive meaning you can create the tour you want to suit where you are on any particular day and will enhance any trip to London for first-time visitors or seasoned Londoners.

We do hope you enjoy exploring the crime movie locations of London, and you never know you may come across them filming a new one!

1
GANG CRIME

In the 2000s the gangster movie sub-genre really took off and this was thought to be the richest time for such movies. However, the idea of portraying gangsters as heroic figures is an old trope and goes back to early films such as *Scar Face* (1932) and *Little Caesar* (1931). These movies depicted the gangsters as underdogs battling with the hand that they were dealt, whereas as time has progressed we have moved through true life violence (*The Krays*) to comedic gangs who are heroes for their ineptitude (*Snatch*).

A Fish Called Wanda (1988)

Dir. Charles Crichton

Aubrey House, 7 Maida Avenue, W2 1TQ
Aubrey House was styled as Kipling Mansions, where Ken Pile (Michael Palin) lived and where Otto (Kevin Kline) was very unkind to fish.

37-38 Hatton Garden, EC1N 8EB
The jewel robbery was to take place at Diamond House. We see Wanda Gershwitz (Jamie Lee Curtis) checking out the site.

37-38 Hatton Garden, EC1N 8EB

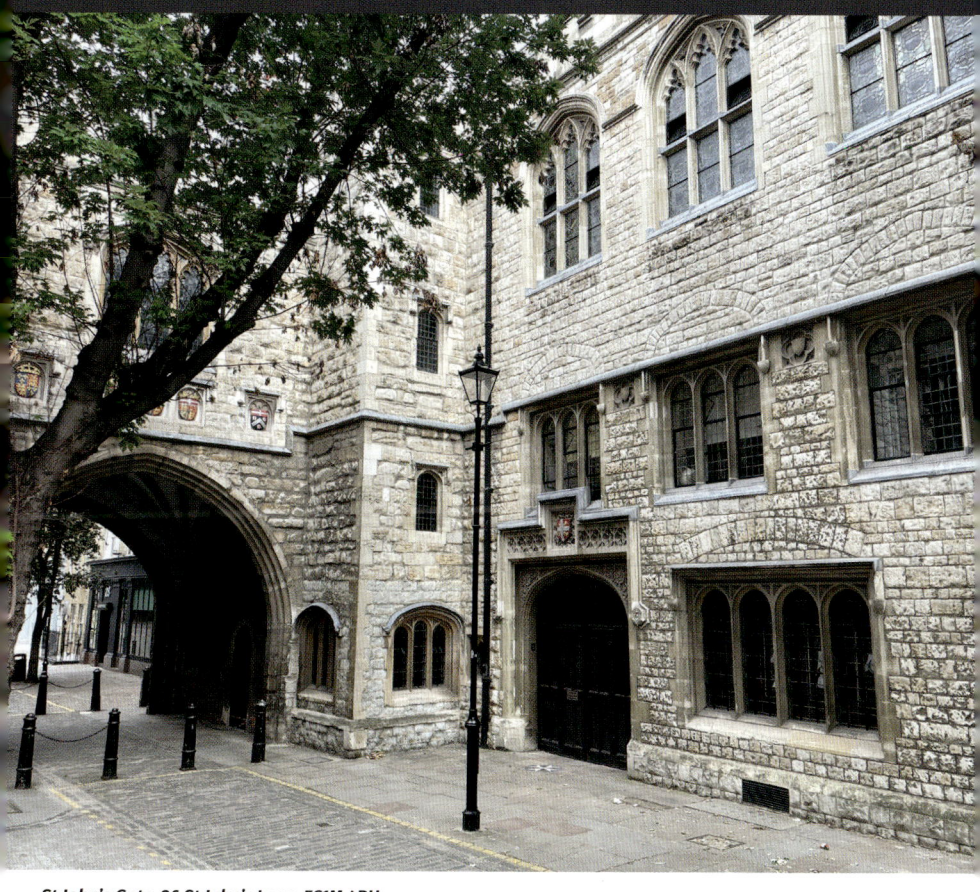

St John's Gate, 26 St John's Lane, EC1M 4BU

Clerkenwell Green, EC1R 0DU
Wanda, as the getaway driver, disguised with a false moustache waits in the car in Clerkenwell but is unfortunately spotted by a dog walker, Mrs Coady (Patricia Hayes).

Robert's Place, Clerkenwell, EC1R 0BB
Following the robbery, the robbers change cars near the steps joining Robert's Place and Clerkenwell Close.

St John's Gate, 26 St John's Lane, EC1M 4BU
Ken Pile (Michael Palin) disposes of the evidence near St John's gate.

69 Onslow Gardens, South Kensington, SW7 3QD
Mrs Coady returns to her home on Onslow Gardens with her dog. Ken makes a bungled attempt on her life.

2 New Square, Lincoln's Inn, WC2A 3RJ
Barrister Archie Leach (John Cleese) had his offices in New Square. This is where Wanda pays him an uncomfortable visit.

New Concordia Wharf, 3 Mill Street, SE1 2BG
Archie Leach borrows a luxurious apartment for his liaison with Wanda, known as St Trevor's Walk. This was actually filmed at New Concordia Wharf.

Legend (2015)

Dir. Brian Helgeland

16 Whittlesey Street, Lambeth, SE1 8SZ
The real Kray twins lived at 178 Vallance Road in Bethnal Green, but this street has long been redeveloped so Whittlesey Street was used instead in this film. Reggie Kray (Tom Hardy) brings tea out for the policemen staking out the property.

The church and the gasometer at the ends of the street were put in digitally in post-production.

32 Caradoc Street, SE10 9AG
Reggie's future wife Frances (Emily Browning) lives here with her brother Frank (Colin Morgan) and her mother (Tara Fitzgerald).

The Long Block, Gibson Gardens, Hackney, N16 7HD
Reggie disappears down an alley on The Long Block and is closely followed by Detective Superintendent Read (Christopher Eccleston).

16 Whittlesey Street, Lambeth, SE1 8SZ

Gatehouse Block, Gibson Gardens, N16 7HL

At the end of the alley, amongst hanging washing, Detective Superintendent Read chases Reggie.

This was filmed at the rear of the Gatehouse Block.

The Ivy House, 40 Stuart Road, Peckham, SE15 3BE

www.ivyhousenunhead.co.uk

Reggie takes Frances to The Double R Club in a bid to impress her and it is here they have their first kiss. She is excited when she spots Joan Collins in the crowd.

The Ivy House is London's first co-operatively owned pub. It is Grade II listed and boasts a number of original 1930s features.

Pellicci's Café, 332 Bethnal Green Road, E2 0AG

This was where the Krays held peace talks with rival gang, the Richardsons. Cornell calls Ronnie a 'Fat Poof' and Reggie just about stops Ronnie from retaliating.

This café has remained almost unchanged since the 1940s and was a place the where the Krays went in real life.

Turner's Old Star, 14 Watts Street, E1W 2QG

www.turnersoldstar.co.uk

Turner's Old Star was used for the Pig and Whistle where a discussion between the Krays and Richardsons quickly descended into a punch up.

Ronnie feigns leaving as he is disappointed the Richardsons brought 'rolling pins' rather than guns. He returns with two hammers.

The pub used to be owned by J.W. Turner the painter. The Old Star is open daily for drinks.

Queen Alexandra's House, Kensington Gore, SW7 2QT

The office of the Krays' business partner, Leslie Payne (David Thewlis) was filmed here, and was where they gently ask a nightclub owner to sell his business, Esmerelda's Barn.

Rivoli Ballroom, 350 Brockley Road, Brockley, SE4 2BY

The Krays' 'new' casino, Esmeralda's Barn, in Knightsbridge was filmed at the Rivoli Ballroom.

The Rivoli was originally built as a picture palace in 1913, and now is the only intact 1950s ballroom in London.

Corner of Teesdale Street & Canrobert Street, E2 6PU

Reggie goes looking for Frances following the fight between the brothers in the club, just after Reggie gets out of prison. He is seen walking down a street market on Teesdale Street.

They changed the appearance of the buildings to look rundown, as it would have looked in in the 1960s.

Coronet Street, between Hoxton Square and Boot Street, N1 6HD
Reggie and Frances walk through the West End at Christmas, and he shows her the Hide-A-Way club. He was in the process of buying it after convincing the owner to sell. This was filmed on Coronet Street.

Café de Paris, 3 Coventry Street, W1D 6BL
The interior shots of The Hide-A-Way were filmed at the Café de Paris which closed in 2020 after standing on the site for nearly a century.

The Café de Paris opened in 1924 and was a popular club with celebrities until it closed. At the end of 2022 it was announced that the venue would reopen in February 2023 under the new name Lío London.

St Anne's Church, Three Colt Street, E14 7HJ
This is where Reggie and Frances got married.

This was a Nicholas Hawksmoor church consecrated in 1730 and is a Grade I listed building. The church is open to visitors Thursday - Saturday but check there are no events going on.

Cedra Court, Cazenove Road, N16 6AT
The newlywed couple lived in a flat in Cedra Court, where in real life the Krays owned a couple of flats, one above the other. In the film Reggie presents Frances with a Triumph Spitfire, even though she couldn't drive, as a gift in front of this building.

The Stag's Head, Orsman Road, N1 5RA
www.stagsheadhoxton.com

Ronnie falls out with Leslie and glasses him in the face. Ronnie was worried that Leslie knew too many 'things' about the Krays and shouldn't be trusted.

They are open daily for drinks and food; they also have regular live music.

The Royal Oak, 73 Columbia Road, E2 7RG
www.royaloakbethnalgreen.co.uk

Ronnie kills George Cornell (Shane Attwooll) in the Blind Beggar for calling him a 'Fat poof'. This was filmed in The Royal Oak on Columbia Road.

The pub is open daily for food and drinks.

2 Theed Street, SE1 8ST
The nervous barmaid (Lorraine Stanley), who witnessed the murder in the Blind Beggar, was walking down Theed Street near number 2, when she sees Reggie and Frances approaching.

James Hammett House, Diss Street, Dorset Estate, E2 7QX
After Frances leaves Reggie following the rape, he goes to Frank's flat on Diss Street to see if she is staying there. He asks her to come back to him, and she refuses. She kills herself not long after in her bedroom.

GANG CRIME | 19

2 Theed Street, SE1 8ST

11 Highbury Hill, Islington, N5 1SU
After falling out with their business partner, Leslie Payne, Jack 'the Hat' McVitie (Sam Spruell) was paid by Ronnie Kray to kill him. The attempt was unsuccessful and Leslie was shot in the leg as Jack flees.

St Peter's Church, St Peter's Close, Bethnal Green, E2 7AE
Jack's body was left outside St Peter's Church, which was a stand in for St Mary's Church in Rotherhithe.

Lock Stock and Two Smoking Barrels (1998)

Dir. Guy Ritchie

Pedley Street, Shoreditch, E1 5FQ
The opening scene shows Eddie (Nick Moran) and Bacon (Jason Statham) running down some steps at speed. This was filmed at the end of Fleet Street Hill tunnel off Pedley Street.

The staircase is still there but in 2018 it was refurbished, replacing the brickwork with railings to make it more open.

38-42 St John Street, Smithfield, EC1M 4DL
Eddie's dad JD (Sting) owned this bar, known simply as JD's.

The building was originally called Vic Naylor's bar and is now EH Smith Design Centre.

Royal Oak Pub, 73 Columbia Road, E2 7RG
www.royaloakbethnalgreen.co.uk

'Samoan Jo's', the South Seas themed pub was filmed at The Royal Oak. Bacon is served 'a f**ing rainforest. You could fall in love with an orangutan in that'.

38-42 St John Street, Smithfield, EC1M 4DL

As a working pub you can of course get a refreshing drink here. But be careful who you talk to when they are watching TV.

Repton Boxing Club, Cheshire Street, Shoreditch, E2 6EG
The disastrous card game took place here, where Eddie loses £500,000 and starts the whole nightmare that is the plot of the film.

Blackman's Shoes, Cheshire Street, Shoreditch, E2 6EH
The exterior shots of 'Hatchet' Harry's (P.H. Moriarty) office were filmed next to Blackman's Shoes, on the corner of Grimsby Street.

Bethnal Green Town Hall, Cambridge Heath Road, E2 9NF
The interior shots of 'Hachet' Harry's office were filmed inside Bethnal Green Town Hall. This has since been turned into a hotel.

13 Park Street, Borough, SE1 9AB
The taxi firm next to the flat where Tom (Jason Flemyng) and Eddie lived was filmed here. Here they planned the robbery and had the unfortunate experience of returning to a room full of bodies.

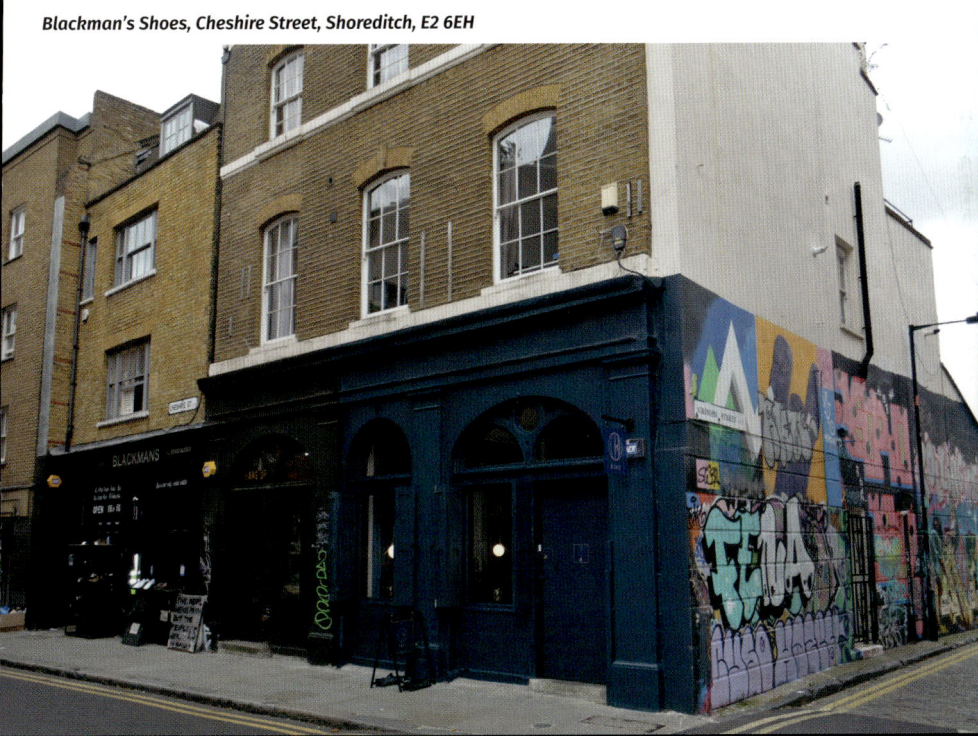

Blackman's Shoes, Cheshire Street, Shoreditch, E2 6EH

13 Park Street, Borough, SE1 9AB

Battersea Bridge, Battersea Bridge Road, SW10 0DQ
Tom is left hanging over Battersea Bridge trying to reach the guns with his ringing mobile in his mouth when the film ends.

London Boulevard (2010)

Dir. Michael Monahan

HMP Pentonville, Caledonian Road, N7 8TT
Mitchel (Colin Farrell) is released from prison and meets up with Billy Norton (Ben Chaplin) outside.

Doyles Tavern, 359 Pentonville Road, N7 9DQ
www.doylestavern.co.uk

Billy waits for Mitchel opposite the prison outside the pub.
    This pub is open daily for drinks as well as showing all major sporting events.

Corner of Mountford Place & Kennington Road, SE11 4DB
They drive off together down Wheelwright Street to the corner of Mountford Place.

Oval Tube Station, Corner of Clapham Road and Harleyford Road, SE11 4PP
Mitchel leaves Oval tube station on his way to his coming out of prison party.

Hanover Arms, 326 Kennington Park Road, SE11 4PP
Mitchel meets Danny (Stephen Graham) and Billy in the pub for his party.
    This pub is open daily for food and drinks.

68 Addison Road, W14 8JL
This was where the external shots for Charlotte's (Keira Knightley) flat were taken. In one scene Mitchel sees a photographer outside her flat, and in another he meets with Charlotte and Jordan (David Thewlis) here.

29 Somerset Square, W14 8EF
The paparazzi were camped out on the roof of this building as they kept an eye on Charlotte's flat on Addison Road. This address is opposite her flat.

Botts Mews, W2 5AG
Mitchel is offered a job as a maintenance man, but the old maintenance man shows up and he is no longer needed. However, a fight breaks out between him and Jordan. The gates were props used for the movie.
    In the film this all took place at the back of Addison Road, which is a small mews off 3 Chepstow Road.
    It was on this road that Mitchel also picks up Charlotte and Jordan for a dental appointment and is later stabbed by the youths who killed Joe.

Botts Mews, W2 5AG

18 Pottery Lane, W11 4LZ

18 Pottery Lane, W11 4LZ
Mitchel ends up getting in a shouting match as the maintenance man approaches him in his van on this road.

Sirinham Point, 4 Meadow Road, SW8 1QB
Mitchel meets Billy to do a bit of debt collection. The wall and steps which can be seen in the scene are no longer there.

98 Holland Park Avenue, W11 3RB
Charlotte goes out in disguise to buy some sanitary products but leaves the shop without them. She can be seen crossing the road here.

Unit 3, 2A Southwark Bridge Road, Bankside, SE1 9HA
Joe (Alan Williams) gets beaten up by a group of kids in the tunnel here. The Eat Restaurant can be seen in the background - this is now a Pret a Manger.

Camberwell New Cemetery, SE23 3RD
Joe is buried at Camberwell New Cemetery. The funeral is attended by Mitchel, Charlotte and Dr Raju (Sanjeev Bhaskar).

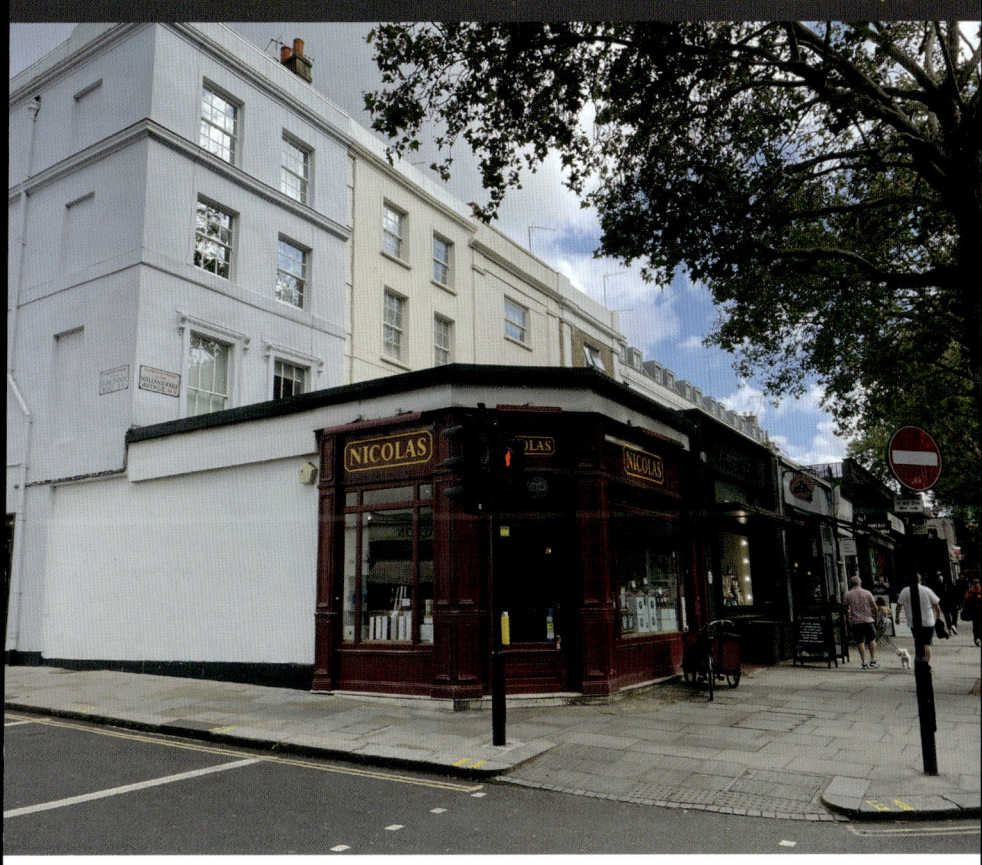

98 Holland Park Avenue, W11 3RB

Criterion, 224 Piccadilly, St James's, W1J 9HP
www.criterion-theatre.co.uk

Mitchel has dinner with Gant (Ray Winstone) in the Criterion restaurant. He turns down the deal and then leaves onto Piccadilly where he sees a large image of Charlotte on the LED display hoardings.

The Criterion was opened in 1874 and is one of the few remaining independent theatres in London.

Weavers Field Playground, 15 Kelsey Street, E2 6HD
The teenagers that killed Joe walk through though Weavers Field Playground.

27 Bartholomew Street, SE1 4AL
Mitchel stops Charlotte's husband's Rolls-Royce outside a café on Bartholomew Street. The Spit and Sawdust pub can just be seen in the background.

27 Bartholomew Street, SE1 4AL

Spit and Sawdust, 21 Bartholomew Street, SE1 4AL
www.spitandsawdust.pub

Mitchel enters the Spit and Sawdust and beats Billy Norton in order to extract information about how Gant knows so much about him. He then steals the money Billy had collected for Gant.

The Spit and Sawdust is open daily for food and drink.

9 Dulwich Village, SE21 7BU
Mitchel walks to Gant's house, where he punches his wife in the face knocking her out. Gant is in bed and Mitchel keeps a gun on him as he gets the box containing £60,000. He hands the box over before Mitchel kills him.

Spit and Sawdust, 21 Bartholomew Street, SE1 4AL

Snatch (2000)

Dir. Guy Ritchie

Ye Olde Mitre Tavern, 1 Ely Court, EC1N 6SJ

www.yeoldemitreholborn.co.uk

Doug 'the Head's' (Mike Reid) local was the Ye Olde Mitre Tavern. In one scene Guy Ritchie, the director, makes an appearance as 'man reading newspaper'.

The pub is unusually officially part of the county of Cambridgeshire, due to being built in 1547 for the servants of the palace of the Bishops of Ely, Cambridgeshire. Although in London, officially it isn't, and it is rumoured that the Metropolitan Police can't enter without permission. Also, the pub boasts an old wooden cherry tree stump and it is believed Elizabeth I danced around it.

Ye Olde Mitre Tavern is open Monday to Friday for food and drink and is closed at the weekend.

Premier House, 12-13 Hatton Garden, EC1N 8AN

The diamond store belonging to Doug 'the Head' was filmed here.

88 Teesdale Street, E2 6QF

Sol's (Lennie James) pawn shop was on Teesdale Road, and where they ended up chopping a man up and the squeaky dog scoffs down the diamond.

Reels Amusements, 127 Broadway, West Ealing, W13 9BE

Reels Amusements was the games arcade and office of Turkish (Jason Statham) which subsequently gets destroyed.

At the time of filming, it was called Jester's Amusements.

14 Tees Avenue, Perivale, UB6 8JH

At the home of Boris the Blade (Rade Šerbedžija) on Tees Avenue, the American and his henchmen look for the diamond, with Boris in the boot of the car.

15 Orsman Road, N1 5RA

Bullet Tooth Tony (Vinnie Jones) crashes the car after his windshield is covered in milkshake on Orsman Road. This enables Boris the Blade to escape from the car briefly before he gets run over by Tyrone (Ade).

Always remember your Green Cross Code people.

Jolly Gardeners, 49-51 Black Prince Road, SE11 6AB

www.thejollygardeners.co.uk

Bullet-Tooth Tony is confronted by Sol and his gang at the Drowning Trout pub.

The pub was originally the Jolly Gardeners, then it was briefly a German gastropub called Zeitgeist. It has since reopened as a community pub once more called the Jolly Gardeners which is open daily for food and drink.

Rosie O'Grady's, 204 Manor Place, SE17 3BN

Outside Rosie O'Grady's pub Franky 'Four Fingers' (Benicio Del Toro) was preparing to enter the bookmakers when he gets trapped in the back of his van when Tyrone parked their car near it. They were hoping to see Franky come out of the bookies but trap him instead.

It is also arguably the best part in the film, when the dog eats the squeaky toy. This pub has since closed down.

The Gentlemen (2020)

Dir. Guy Ritchie

Princess Victoria, 217 Uxbridge Road, W12 9DH
www.princessvictoria.co.uk

This is the headquarters of the so-called 'king of the jungle' Mickey Pearson (Matthew McConaughey). He appears to be assassinated in the first scene here, and then later in the film it was where Dry Eye approached him in order to buy him out of the business.

The pub was built in 1829 as a gin palace and has overnight accommodation. It is open daily for food and drink but may not serve pickled eggs.

Tate Modern, Boiler House, East Room, Bankside, SE1 9TG

The office of the *Daily Print* newspaper was filmed in the East Room at the Tate Modern. This was where Fletcher (Hugh Grant) meets with Big Dave (Eddie Marson), to discuss uncovering Mickey's dealings.

The Euro Café, 299 Caledonian Road, Islington, N1 1DT

Coach (Colin Farrell) is introduced to the film in a café when a group of youths come in causing trouble. He teaches them a much-needed lesson and tells them to come to his gym for proper training.

Repton Boxing Club, 116 Cheshire Street, E2 6EG

Coach's boxing gym is filmed at the Repton Boxing Club where the Toddlers

Repton Boxing Club, Cheshire Street, Shoreditch, E2 6EG

train and where they bring the weed from their raid on Mickey's farm.

Annabel's, 46 Berkeley Square, Mayfair, W1J 5AT
Mickey and Matthew (Jeremy Strong) meet after the farm had been raided by the Toddlers at Annabel's in Berkeley Square. Matthew gives Mickey a gift of a paperweight showing the deal is still on.

Annabel's opened in 1963 in the basement of 44 Berkeley Square – the Clermont Club – but has since moved.

Lancresse Court, De Beauvoir Town, N1 5TG
Ray (Charlie Hunnam) goes to Lancresse Court to take Laura Pressfield (Eliot Sumner) home from the 'south-London high-rise'. Things don't go according to plan when the son of a Russian oligarch accidentally falls out of a window.

Corbiere House, Balmes Road, N1 5SR
Ray chases the kids who saw the oligarch's son fall from the window. They were filming the incident and Ray makes it clear he wants their phones. He ends up in a confrontation in the garages on Balmes Road when one of the lads pulls a machete out, which is trumped by Ray's automatic weapon.

King's Head, Poplar Place, Bayswater, W2 4AH
Coach tells Ray about the guy, Phuc (James Wong), who is in the boot of his car. Phuc was the one who gave the Toddlers the location of Mickey's farm. This was filmed outside the King's Head.

Fen Shang Princess, Southern Star Cumberland Basin, Prince Albert Road, NW1 7SS
Lord George (Tom Wu) confronts Dry Eye in front of this restaurant about how Phuc went behind his back on Mickey Pearson's farm raid.

Emirates Stadium, Arsenal Football Club, 75 Hornsey Road, N7 7AJ
Dry Eye meets Matthew for a confidential talk in the stands, but Fletcher filmed it and got a lip reader to transcribe what was said.

Brompton Cemetery, Old Brompton Road, SW5 9JE
Dry Eye talks to his uncle in the car as part of his plan to take over Mickey's business. This was filmed on the main thoroughfare through the centre of the cemetery with the domed chapel in the background.

23 Warple Way, Acton, W3 0RX
After Mickey and Ray get hit by a truck Mickey gets out of the car and runs down Warple Way.

New Billingsgate Fish Market, Trafalgar Way, E14 5ST
Mickey has a conversation with Matthew at the Billingsgate Fish Market

where Matthew asks for a reduction in the cost of buying the business.

Mickey shows him the frozen body of Dry Eye to show he's not ready to renegotiate the deal and is in fact two steps ahead of him.

4 Spring Bridge Road, Ealing, W5 2AA
Mail Boxes Etc. where Fletcher (Hugh Grant) had stored all the evidence of the business transactions was filmed here.

Neo Bankside, 72 Holland Street, SE1 9NX
After Fletcher pitches his script to Miramax, he jumps into a taxi outside the studios to take him to the airport. Sadly, he doesn't quite make it.

This was filmed on the corner of Holland Street and Castle Yard.

The Hatton Garden Job (2017)

Dir. Ronnie Thompson

St Mary the Virgin Church, 1 Langley Drive, E11 2LN
Danny (Phil Daniels) meets with Brian Reader (Larry Lamb) in the cemetery of this church to see if he is interested in taking part in The Hatton Garden Job. Initially he says 'no' as he thinks he is too old.

The Railway Tavern Hotel, 131 Angel Lane, E15 1DB
www.the-railway-tavern-hotel.business.site

Brian Reader, Danny Jones and 'XXX' (Matthew Goode) meet to discuss The Hatton Garden Job and who else will be involved.

This pub is open daily for drinks and 24 hours on Friday and Saturday.

88-90 Hatton Garden, EC1N 8PN
The burglary took place at this site. All the external shots were filmed here. This is the site of the real robbery that the film is based on.

Bernelių Užeiga, Shepherd's Inn, 485 High Road, Leytonstone, E11 4PG
www.berneliaiuk.co.uk

This is where XXX meets Erzebet Zslondos (Joely Richardson) to get the codes for the alarms in 88-90 Hatton Garden.

This is now a Lithuanian restaurant.

1 West India Quay, 26 Hertsmere Road, E14 4EG
An external shot of 1 West India Quay, which has been made to look like Isaac's Casino where Erzebet Zslondos bumps into Marcus Ford (Stephen Moyer) was filmed here.

371 Mount Pleasant, WC1X 0BD
XXX is picked up by Baskin (Mark Cooper Harris) in his car and they drive away. You can see the Oriental Taste in the background from a viewpoint in Mount Pleasant.

88-90 Hatton Garden, EC1N 8PN

The Apple Tree, 45 Mount Pleasant, WC1X 0AE
www.theappletreelondon.com

You can see The Apple Tree pub in the background as Baskin drops XXX off.

It is seen from Phoenix Place looking back, with the white sorting office on the left.

At the time of writing the pub was temporarily closed.

Hat & Mitre Court, EC1M 4EF
Just before the job starts on Hatton Garden we see the white transit reverse into Hat & Mitre Court looking out onto St John Street.

14 St Cross Street, EC1N 8UN
In a small alley down the side of 14 St Cross Street, we see XXX make a call to get a lift from Judas Jack (Jack Doolan) following the robbery.

GANG CRIME | 33

371 Mount Pleasant, WC1X 0BD

Hat and Mitre Court, EC1M 4EF

467 High Street, Leytonstone, E11 4JU
Following the handover of the box to Frank, XXX walks past this travel agent and disappears as a bus passes, making the viewer assume he left the country.

The Krays (1990)

Dir. Peter Medak

32 Caradoc Street, SE10 9AG
The Krays' family home was represented by 32 Caradoc Street. The garden was also used as the house of Reggie's (Martin Kemp), soon to be wife Frances (Kate Hardie).

The Krays' family home was originally 178 Vallance Road, Bethnal Green, but this has been redeveloped since the 1960s.

Thornley Place, SE10 9AF
The street scenes of Bethnal Green in the Second World War, when the police were looking for the Krays' father, Charlie Kray (Alfred Lynch) were filmed on Thornley Place.

Aldwych Station, Surrey Street, WC2R 2ND
www.ltmuseum.co.uk/hidden-london

Vi (Billie Whitelaw) takes the boys down to Bethnal Green tube station during an air raid. This shelter was filmed at the disused Aldwych Station.

Aldwych Station was officially closed in 1994, as it was not cost effective to renovate it and install accessible lifts. However, it has been used as a filming location since then and is occasionally opened to the public for specialist tours run by the London Transport Museum.

Hackney Free Parochial School, 39 Wilton Way, E8 3ED

The Kray twins attended school at the Hackney Free Parochial School on Wilton Way and started their bullying in the playground.

This building has been renovated into flats, although the exterior has been mostly retained.

Richmond Theatre, 1 Little Green, Richmond, TW9 1QH

www.atgtickets.com/venues/richmond-theatre

The external shots of the nightclub, the Regal Club, run by the Ronnie (Gary Kemp) and Reggie Kray (Martin Kemp) was filmed at the Richmond Theatre.

Designed by architect Frank Matcham the Richmond Theatre was opened in 1899. It has been an active cinema since it opened.

Wilton's Music Hall, 1 Graces Alley, Whitechapel, E1 8JB

www.wiltons.org.uk

The interior shots of the Regal Club (and the snooker hall) were filmed at Wilton's Music Hall.

Wilton's Music Hall was built in 1859 by architect Jacob Maggs and has had an interesting history. It caught fire in 1878 and had to be rebuilt. It is one of the few saloon-style music halls still in its original form and was reopened as a performance venue in 1997.

Royal Oak Pub, 73 Columbia Road, E2 7RG

www.royaloakbethnalgreen.co.uk

The Kray twins and their gang enter the Royal Oak pub and pepper the entire bar with bullets.

As a working pub today, it is nowhere near as terrifying as this scene would suggest.

The pub is open daily for food and drinks.

Fleece House, 160 Abbey Street, SE1 3NR

George Cornell (Steven Berkoff) taunts Ronnie's boyfriend Steve (Gary Love), claiming Ronnie is 'tied to his mother's apron strings' in this pub.

Later in the film Jack 'the Hat' (Tom Bell) gets plastered here and is evicted from the bar. He is then seen walking past the Marquis of Wellington, Druid Street, to his final scene.

Walcot Stores, 68 Walcot Square, SE11 4UH

Reggie overreacts as two men admire both his car and Frances when he is in the Walcot Stores. He gives them a beating as the hysterical Frances looks on.

The shop is also used for the scene where Frances Kray (Kate Hardie) is given specialist treatment in the shop even though she doesn't ask for, want or expect it.

Watergate Street, SE8 3HH
Jack 'the Hat' McVitie pushes his girlfriend (Soo Drouet) out of his moving car on this street. She had made comments that he was bald (he was), and he therefore left her for dead in the road.

Café de Paris, 3–4 Coventry Street, W1D 6BL
The Krays were photographed with Judy (Julia Migenes) inside this nightclub. This is likely to have been Judy Garland who was famously acquainted with the Krays.

The Café de Paris opened in 1924 and was a popular club with celebrities until it closed in 2020. At the end of 2022 it was announced that the venue would reopen in February 2023 under the new name Lío London.

The Bacchus, 177 Hoxton Street, N1 6PJ
This pub represented the Blind Beggar pub where Ronnie Kray killed George Cornell (Steven Berkoff) by shooting him in the face.

This bar was refurbished into the Superheroes Bar, a comic book inspired

Café de Paris, 3–4 Coventry Street, W1D 6BL

bar serving drinks and afternoon tea but is now The Bacchus bar.

Woolwich Cemetery, Camdale Road, SE18 2DS
The Krays' mum Violet was buried at Woolwich Cemetery. Both brothers were given leave from prison for the funeral and are seen standing by the grave with a police officer on either side of them.

Paddington Station, Praed Street, W2 1HB

The Long Good Friday (1980)

Dir. John Mackenzie

St George-in-the-East Church, Cannon Street Road, E1 0BH
Harold Shand's (Bob Hoskin's) mum nearly gets blown up here during the Good Friday service. The exterior shots were taken at St-George-in-the-East.

This church was built between 1714 and 1729 by Nicholas Hawksmoor. The original interior of the church was damaged when it was hit by a bomb in the Blitz and was replaced in the 1960s.

St Patrick's Church, The Presbytery, Dundee Street, E1W 2PH

The interior shots of the Good Friday service were filmed at St Patrick's Church.

The Salisbury, 1 Green Lanes, Haringey Ladder, N4 1JX

www.thesalisburyhotelpub.co.uk

This was the location of Fagan's Irish Pub where Colin (Paul Freeman) hits on the doomed Irish boy (Kevin McNally).

The Salisbury currently offer food and drink.

Paddington Station, Praed Street, W2 1HB

Carol Benson (Patti Love) collects her husband's body (Leo Dolan) from the railway station.

The Aegean Pools, 2 Hale Lane, Mill Hill, NW7 3NX

This was the diving pool where Colin is diving before being killed by Pierce Brosnan's unnamed character.

The Aegean is no longer a pool and is instead an Argentine restaurant.

Ladywell Leisure Centre, 261 Lewisham High Street, SE13 6AY

Colin's murder took place here.

The Leisure Centre is no longer there and has been replaced with a colourful residential/commercial space.

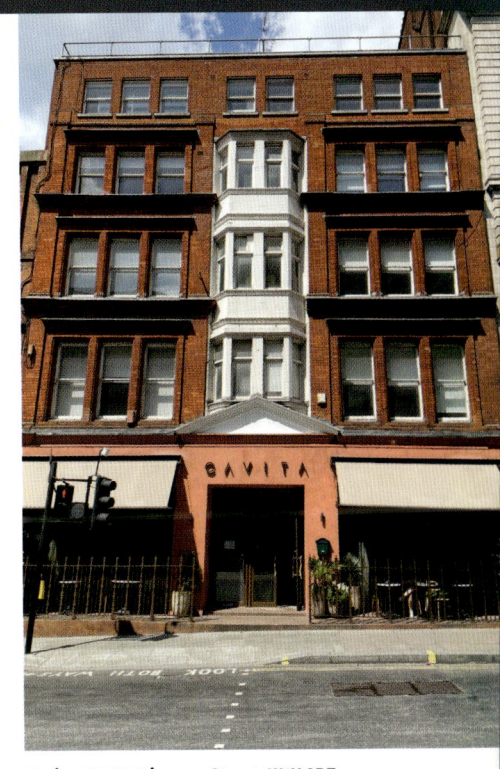

Cavita, 56-60 Wigmore Street, W1U 2RZ

33 Villa Road, Brixton, SW9 7ND

The house of Erroll 'the Grass' (Paul Barber), who gets cut up by 'Razors' (P.H. Moriarty) was filmed here.

Cavita, 56-60 Wigmore Street, W1U 2RZ

Jeff (Derek Thompson) gets spat on when he is having dinner with Councillor Harris (Bryan Marshall).

This restaurant is now Cavita.

The Waterman's Arms, 1 Glenaffric Avenue, E14 3BW

www.thewatermansarms.co.uk

Savoy, Strand, WC2R 0EZ

The interior shots of the 'Governor General Pub' were filmed at the Waterman's Arms. It is here that Harold, finds Billy (Nick Stringer) and tells him to walk to the car.

The pub is open daily for food and drink.

15 Catherine Place, SW1E 6DX
This private residence was used for the exterior shots of Harold's Casino.

The Savoy, The Strand, WC2R 0EZ
The Mafia contacts all stay at The Savoy hotel, where Harold is abducted before being dumped and then kidnapped by the IRA.

St Katharine's Dock, 50 St Katharine's Way, E1W 1LA
The boat where Harold and Victoria (Helen Mirren) entertain the American contacts was moored at St Katharine's Dock.

99 Kensington High Street, (Kensington Roof Gardens), W8 5SA
Victoria has dinner in a restaurant here where she tries to tell the American contacts that bomb explosions are all a normal day's work for her.

King George V Dock, E16 2LH
Harold stands at the quayside here and gets the name of the grass from his contact the bent copper, Parky (Dave King).

2 ROBBERIES

Many recent British robbery and heist movies are based on true events, such as the Hatton Garden heist, the Brink's-Mat robbery, and Baker Street bank job. Although embellished and changed for artistic purposes real-life crimes still fascinate us more than those which are purely fiction. In fact, the first crime film ever was *The Great Train Robbery* (1903) which was loosely based on railroad theft in the American West.

11 Harrowhouse (1974)

Dir. Aram Avakian

Annabel's, 46 Berkeley Square, W1J 5AT
Berkeley Square was the location of 11 Harrowhouse, and in the early scenes we see Meecham (John Gielgud) speaking with Coglin (Peter Vaughan) outside on the steps.

They also filmed in the square itself under the pavilion when Howard met with Charles D. Watts (James Mason) to discuss the heist.

31 Blomfield Road, W9 1AA
Howard and Maren Shirell (Candice Bergen) go to Antwerp to visit a diamond merchant, although this was actually filmed in Little Venice.

101 Dalmatians (1996)

Dir. Stephen Herek

46/48 Palace Gardens Terrace, W8 4PX
Roger Dearly (Jeff Daniels) lives at this house and the opening scenes show Pongo getting him up in the morning.

Minster Court, Mincing Lane, EC3R 7BD
The fashion house, the House of DeVil, belonging Cruella de Vil (Glenn Close) was filmed at Minster Court.

Montage
There is a delightful montage around London, with Roger Dearly and Anita (Joely Richardson) being led on their bikes around the city.

- Leicester Square, WC2H 7AL – Pongo chaotically pulls Roger on his bike through the square, in contrast to Anita cycling sedately with Perdita.
- Trafalgar Square, WC2N 5DN

ROBBERIES | 41

Burlington Arcade, 51 Piccadilly, W1J 0QJ

- Burlington Arcade, 51 Piccadilly, W1J 0QJ
- Jermyn Street, SW1Y 6ST
- Duke of York Column and Steps, SW1Y 5AJ
- St James's Park, SW1A 2BJ - Roger cycles through the park and ends up in the lake.

Hyde Park Bandstand, W2 2UH
After meeting Anita they both cycle past the Hyde Park bandstand which was built in 1886.

Battersea Park, SW11 4NJ
Many of the St James's Park scenes were filmed in the quieter Battersea Park.

Parish Church of St Luke, Sydney Street, SW3 6NH
Roger and Anita get married in this church with all their dogs and four-legged friends at the back and waiting outside.

38 Stoney Street, Borough, SE1 9LB
Jasper (Hugh Laurie) and Horace (Mark Williams), visit the taxidermist Skinner (John Shrapnel) on Stoney Street. Jasper tells Horace not to talk and not to look at Skinner's scar. Once the door is opened, he does both.
Stoney Street has since been refurbished but the railway arch is still in place.

102 Dalmatians (2000)

Dir. Kevin Lima

Westminster Bridge, SE1 7GA
Big Ben chiming triggered Cruella's (Glenn Close) hallucinations and before long they instigated her joining forces with Jean-Pierre Le Pelt (Gérard Depardieu).

Wandsworth Youth River Club, Putney Embankment, SW15 1LS
The River Club was used to represent the 'Second Chance' animal shelter run by Kevin Shepherd (Ioan Gruffudd).

Sarum Chase, 23 West Heath Road, Hampstead, NW3 7UU
The exterior shots of Cruella de Vil's house were filmed at Sarum Chase.
The house was built in 1932 for artist, Francis Owen Salisbury. It was also used as a location in the 1960s for a Rolling Stones photo session for *Beggars' Banquet*.

12 Park Street, Borough, SE1 9AB
Cruella's parole officer Chloe Simon (Alice Evans) lived here.

40 Brunswick Gardens, Kensington, W8 4AL
Cruella's butler Alonzo (Tim McInnerny) is stealing puppies from the first floor

ROBBERIES | **43**

of this building before he fell through the floor into the basement.

Hampstead High Street Police Station, 26 Rosslyn Hill, NW3 1PA

Kevin (Ioan Gruffudd) escapes from Hampstead High Street Police Station with help from the talking parrot, Waddlesworth (Eric Idle) after being arrested for dognapping.

The police station has been closed since 2013 and is a Grade II listed building. It was empty at the time of writing.

Left: *Sarum Chase, 23 West Heath Road, Hampstead, NW3 7UU*

Below: *Hampstead High Street Police Station, 26 Rosslyn Hill, NW3 1PA*

St Pancras, Euston Road, N1C 4QP (courtesy of Colin on Wikimedia Commons)

St Pancras Euston Road, N1C 4QP
Cruella and Le Pelt took the Orient Express from St Pancras Station.

However, the Orient Express in reality leaves from Victoria Station not St Pancras.

Bellman and True (1987)

Dir. Richard Loncraine

Paddington Station, Praed Street, W2 1HU
Hiller (Bernard Hill) and his stepson aka The Boy (Kieran O'Brien) leave Paddington Station through the main entrance. They

then turn into Praed Street but they don't realise they are being followed.

43 Leinster Square, W2 4PU
Hiller and The Boy check in at a hotel which is meant to be located in Paddington but is actually in Leinster Square. They are watched from across the road as they enter the hotel.

117 Queensway, W2 4SJ
Brian Gort (Ken Bones) watches Hiller and his stepson as they walk down Queensway, from a phone box opposite Cain Brothers.

Later when Hiller is being chased by Gort they run down Queensway and past Whiteley's Department Store.

Whiteley's opened in 1911, and was closed in 2013 for redevelopment into luxury flats.

Westbourne Grove, W2 4UA
After leaving the newsagents Hiller spots Gort and realises they were being followed. He grabs his stepson and they run down Westbourne Grove, towards Kensington Gardens Square.

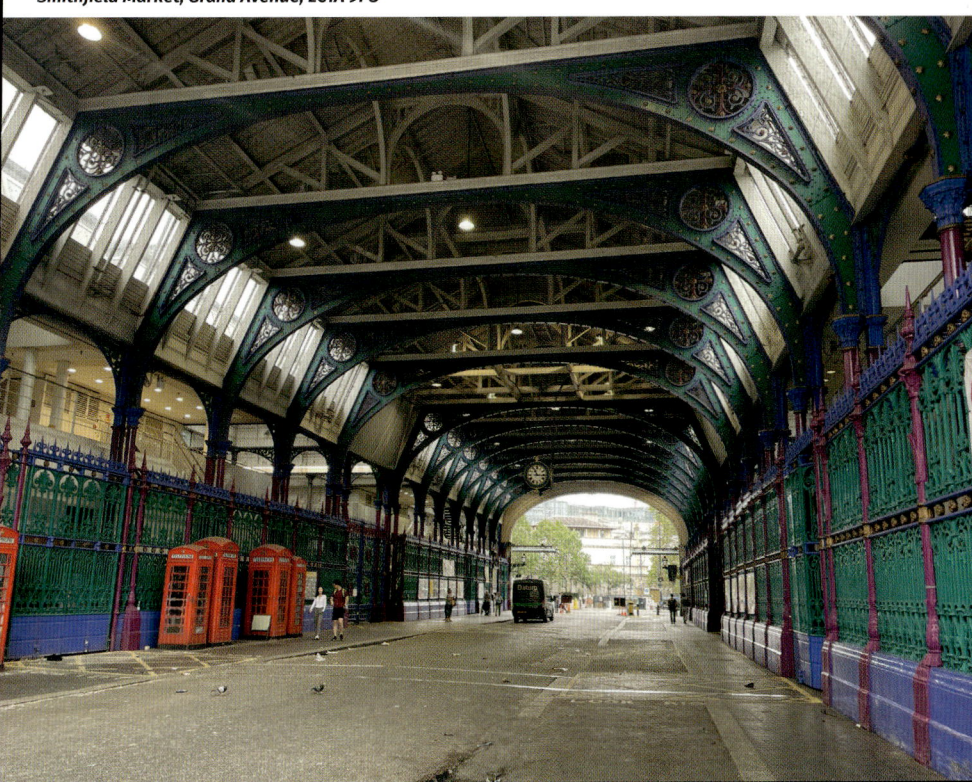

Smithfield Market, Grand Avenue, EC1A 9PS

Aldwych Underground Station, Surrey Street, WC2R 2ND
www.ltmuseum.co.uk/hidden-london

Hiller looks for his stepson as he reaches the tube station. As he runs down the stairs, he is confronted by the man who was watching him outside his hotel.

All the tube station shots were filmed at the long-abandoned Aldwych Underground Station. Aldwych Station was officially closed in 1994, as it was not cost effective to renovate it. However, it has been used as a filming location since then and is occasionally opened to the public for specialist tours run by the London Transport Museum.

16 Charles Street, W1J 5DS
The cab stops outside a gaming club which in the film is covered in scaffolding. This is 16 Charles Street and may very well be covered in scaffolding when you visit – such is the nature of London.

Hiller is waiting inside to be reunited with his stepson.

Middle Pond, Hampstead Heath, NW5 1QR
Hiller and Anna (Frances Tomelty) take his stepson to Hampstead Heath, and they launch his model boat onto the Middle Pond. They are watched by Gort.

Smithfield Market, Grand Avenue, EC1A 9PS
Donkey (John Kavanagh) walks through Smithfield Market, with the large clock in the foreground of the shot. He then approaches the Daimler Sovereign, at the entrance looking towards Charterhouse Street.

Buster (1988)

Dir. David Green

Cat and Mutton Pub, 76 Broadway Market, E8 4RA
www.catandmutton.com

At the beginning of the film, Buster Edwards (Phil Collins) walks past this pub after stealing a suit.

This pub was established in 1729 and is open daily for food and drink.

Abady House, Page Street (Grosvenor Estate), SW1P 4EW
Buster Edwards hid out here in his mother-in-law's (Sheila Hancock) flat following the robbery.

Calculated Risk (1967)

Dir. Norman Harrison

HMP Wandsworth, Heathfield Road, SW18 3HU
Kenneth 'Kip' Walton (John Rutland) is released from Wandsworth prison, and we see him leaving by the main entrance.

His brother-in-law Steve Bannerman (William Lucas) is waiting on Heathfield Avenue with the prison in the background.

HMP Wandsworth, Heathfield Road, SW18 3HU (courtesy of geography.org.uk, Wikimedia Commons)

Wandsworth prison was built in 1851 as the Surrey House of Correction as part of the separate system principle and is one of the largest in the UK. The corridors all radiate from a central point.

Isleworth Cemetery, Park Road, Isleworth, TW7 6AZ

Steve and Kip lay flowers on Kip's wife's grave. She died when he was in prison. This was filmed in Isleworth Cemetery. They approach a bench which is to the right of the Pears family memorial.

Northumberland House, Lower Square, Isleworth, TW7 6RL

Steve checks out the location of the robbery and looks into Lower Square with the Northumberland Arms on the left.

The pub closed in 1983 and was converted first to offices and then to apartments. It was also once part of the Old Blue School.

Shepherd's Bush Market, W12 8DF

Simmie (Warren Mitchell) speaks with a market trader here, with the arches in the background to discuss explosives needed for the heist. The Hammersmith and City Line train passes over on the left.

North Street, Isleworth, TW7 6RE

Nodge (Terence Cooper) walks Julie Salting (Dilys Watling) home one evening. They walk along the wall with the park to the right of them. In the shot the White Swan pub is visible in the background but that doesn't seem to be possible in reality.

Above: Northumberland House, Lower Square, Isleworth, TW7 6RL

Below: North Street, Isleworth, TW7 6RE

4 Swan Street, Isleworth, TW7 6XA

4 Swan Street, Isleworth, TW7 6XA
The location of the bank was number 4 Swan Street, facing the corner of North Street. The frontage of the bank was added for the film.

Cockneys vs Zombies (2012)
Dir. Matthias Hoene

Fen Street, E16 1JS
Andy (Harry Treadaway) and Terry (Rasmus Hardiker) meet with Mental Mickey (Bashy) in the underpass on Fen Street to confirm their arrangements for 2pm.

Mickey head butts the bonnet of their car to show the meeting has ended.

135 Bus Stop (MA), Spindrift Avenue, E14 9US
Dave Tuppance (Jack Doolan) is 'staying under the radar' when Andy and Terry catch up with him as he is waiting at this bus stop.

Cubitt Town Library, 52 Strattondale Street, E14 3HG

The Maguires staged their robbery at a bank which was filmed at the Cubitt Town Library. By dressing as construction workers with false moustaches they accidently confuse the bank manager into thinking they were with Heartman Construction. She tries to hand over their loan money.

As the robbers leave, the police are waiting for them resulting in a shootout on the doorstep as Mental Mickey loses his cool.

Leven Road, Poplar, E14 0NB

As they are making their getaway Mickey shoots a zombie in the back of the van, knocking her out the back doors.

The gas towers on the side of the road (opposite the basketball court) where the zombie lands were demolished in 2018, and flats are being built on the site.

1 Huntingdon Street, London Royal Docks, E16 1HS

Emma's (Georgia King) sister's house was filmed on Huntingdon Street. Emma peered over the wall of this residential property before going in.

You can see the church in the background, but the 'Moss Electrical' building, where the football fans are fighting has since been refurbished.

Harbour Square Park, Timber Quay Park, 22 Lovegrove Walk, E14 9PZ

The final scene of the film as the residents from Bowbell's Care Home board the boat following their fight with the zombies was filmed opposite the Docklands Scout Project and south of this park.

Face (1997)

Dir. Antonia Bird

Sandringham Road, Dalston, E8 2LL

Ray (Robert Carlyle) and Connie (Lena Headey) meet during a confrontation on the street.

32 Southwood Lawn Road, Highgate, N6 5SH

Ray and Stevie (Steven Waddington) drive to Southwood Lawn Road where they pick up Dave (Ray Winstone).

Spencer Street, EC1V 0HB

They then drive through London and pass a demonstration on the corner of Spencer Street and Goswell Road.

39 Moreland Street, Clerkenwell, EC1V 8BB

There is a disturbance outside Stepney Green Tube station, but in reality this was filmed on Moreland Street and the Underground signs were props added for the film.

Liverpool Street Underground Station, Liverpool Street, EC2M 1QT
Julian (Phil Davis) meets with Dave outside Liverpool Street Station and walks towards the car.

Billy's Café, 4 Pritchard's Road, Bethnal Green, E2 9AP
The gang walk past Billy's Café on Pritchard's Road and walk down Coate Street with the café clearly visible in the background behind them. There was originally a wall on the left-hand side of Coate Street which has since been demolished.

Later in the film they look from their vantage point down Coate Street with Pritchard's Road at the junction.

370 Bancroft Road, Bethnal Green, E1 4BU
Ray, Dave and Stevie return to the house on Bancroft Road where Ray had stored the cash. Number 370 has the boot scraper near the steps that is clearly seen in the shot.

Dagmar Court, Manchester Road, Isle of Dogs, E14 3JF
The gang head over to the Manchester Road Estate where they consider who they can speak to next.

3-5 Crown Close, Bow, E3 2JH
They walk along the footbridge over the A12 from Crown Close to Wendon Street. As they arrive onto Wendon Street they spots a blonde woman getting into a car.

Liverpool Street Station, Liverpool Street, EC2M 1QT

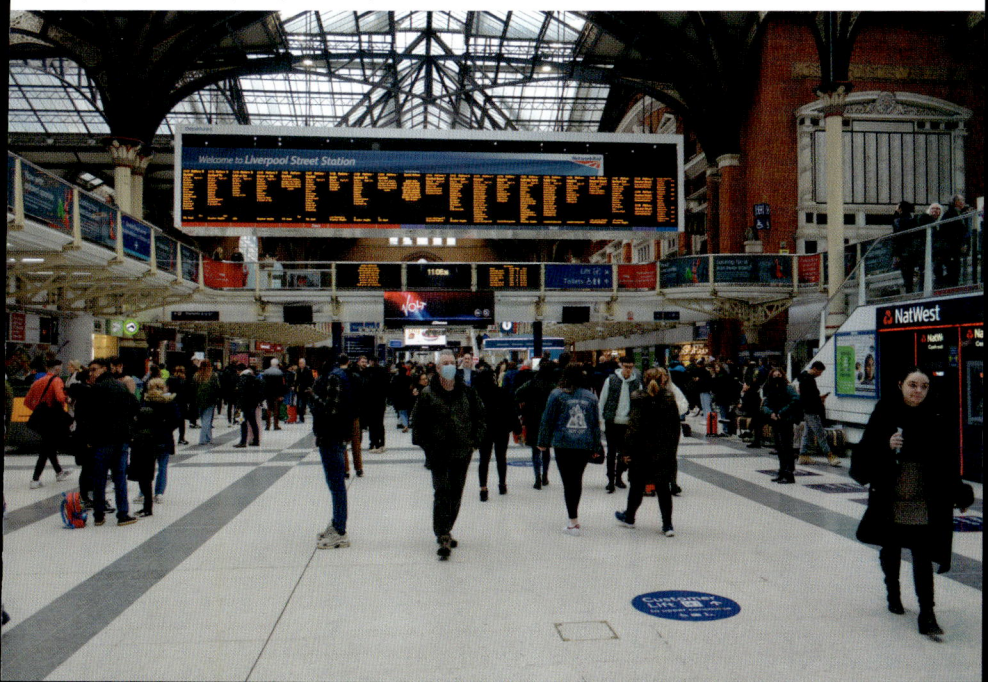

25 Hillfield Park, Muswell Hill, N10 3QT

They park their car on Hillfield Park, more or less outside number 25 with the shot looking downhill. Then they split up on foot as they reach Hillfield Park Mews.

63-65 Mattison Road, N4 1BG

After they make the surprising discovery, they make a run for it and emerge on Mattison Road through Haringey Passage.

South Haringey School, 110 Pemberton Road, Haringey Ladder, N4 1BA

Stevie and Ray try to get though a gaggle of school children, unsurprisingly gathering outside the school gates of South Haringey School.

72 Cheshire Street, E2 6EH

Connie and Ray have an argument which results in them chasing Dave over the pedestrian bridge which runs between Cheshire Street and Pedley Street. Since filming this has become a major location for street art.

Pedley Street, Shoreditch, E1 5FQ

They beat Dave up underneath a railway bridge known as Fleet Street Hill, just off Pedley Street with St Anne's Church clearly illuminated in the background. This was also where the opening scene from *Lock Stock and Two Smoking Barrels* was shot.

Get Lucky (2013)

Dir. Sacha Bennett

Blackwall Tunnel, SE10 0QE

Lucky (Luke Treadaway) and Kirby (Ali Cook) are chased by Sebastian (Craig Fairbrass) and Kramer (Terry Stone) after Kirby steals the money from the safe through the streets of London and through the Blackwall Tunnel, approaching via the decorative arch.

As they emerge from the tunnel you can see the dome in the background.

Millwall Inner Dock, E14 9RD

The river chase following the heist at the private casino takes them through Millwall Inner Dock, through a double leaf bascule bridge.

HQTS Lord Amory, 631 Manchester Road, Docklands, E14 3NU

Then they pass the Docklands Scout Project Lord Amory boat which is the only permanently moored campsite in the UK.

Lucky picks them up in front of the Lord Amory in the black taxi.

King of Thieves (2018)

Dir. James Marsh

Tower Bridge, Tower Bridge Road, SE1 2UP

Brian Reader (Michael Caine) is on the bus heading into Hatton Garden and there is a shot of the bus heading over

Tower Bridge, viewed from Butler's Wharf. The bus continues over the bridge and Minster House on Mincing Lane EC3 is in the centre distance.

88-90 Hatton Garden, EC1N 8PN
Brian and Basil (Charlie Cox) are seen walking past 88-90 Hatton Garden where Basil talks about his connection with the key. The external shots are repeated throughout the movie as the heist takes place here.

The real heist also took place at this site.

Ely Court, Hatton Garden, EC1N 6RY
Brian and Basil pass the entrance to Ely Court on Hatton Garden EC1 with Ye Olde Mitre public house in the background.

Elegance Jewellers, 8-9 Greville Street, EC1N 8SB
Brian talks to Basil about the value of flawless diamonds, a few of which will be stored in the vault overnight. It is meant to be Hatton Garden, but they are walking past Elegance jewellers on Greville Street.

Junction between Tidal Basin Road, and A1011, Silvertown Way, E16 1AD
Danny Jones (Ray Winstone) and Carl Wood (Paul Whitehouse) are driving in the car as they go to meet Brian to talk about the job. Looking south on the A1011 Silvertown Way with traffic signals at the junction of Tidal Basin Way in the left background.

Ely Court, Hatton Garden, EC1N 6RY

24 Hatton Garden, EC1N 8BQ
As they are making the final checks on the plan, Brian is picked up by Kenny (Tom Courtney) in the white Mercedes parked outside number 24 Hatton Garden. Kenny suggests getting a white van, as no one talks to 'gasmen'.

Bank of England, Threadneedle Street, EC3V 3LA
When the hydraulic pump breaks in the middle of the job, they leave in a white van and drive towards the Bank of England. The shot is taken from the corner of Princes Street and

Threadneedle Street, past the Royal Exchange and down Cornhill, and then past the glass Leadenhall Building on Leadenhall Street.

River Café, 14 Station Road Approach, SW6 3UH
Brian meets Basil here and Basil tells him the gang think he has lost his nerve as he pulled out from the job. Basil offers him 50% of anything he gets in exchange for the numbers of the boxes with the most valuable contents.

Porchester Centre, Queensway, W2 5HS
Kenny and Billy (Michael Gambon) were here at the spa, talking about how Kenny has taken over the role of the 'Guv'nor' after Brian left.

The Viaduct, 221 Uxbridge Road, W7 3TD
www.viaduct-hanwell.co.uk

Kenny met Terry Perkins (Jim Broadbent) and Danny Jones at the King's Arms which in reality is the Viaduct.
They are open daily for food and drink.

The Bird in Hand, 88 Masbro Road, Brook Green, W14 0LR
www.thebirdinhandlondon.com

Brian asks to meet the rest of the gang in the pub to discuss the division of the loot to ensure he and Basil get their fair share.
They are open for food and drink every day except Monday.

37 Milson Road, Hammersmith, W14 0LD
Whilst the gang are in the Bird in Hand Pub, the police bug Terry's car which is parked outside number 37 Milson Road.

15 May Gardens, Wembley, HA0 1DU
Danny and Terry buy a smelter from a man who lived at this address and had a broken-down ice-cream van in the front drive.

Fishmonger's Hall Wharf, Thames Path, EC4R 3AE
Brian calls Basil from a payphone on Fishmonger's Hall Wharf. He tells Brian that the gang say they gave him his fair share. The phone box was likely put there for the film. After he finished the phone call, Brian walks towards London Bridge.

London City Airport, Hartmann Road, E16 2PB
Basil decides to run and takes the Docklands Light Railway (DLR) getting off the train at London City Airport. He ditches his phone at the bottom of the escalator.

4 Oakdene, Ealing, W13 8AW
Terry's daughter's house, where Terry, Danny and Kenny are arrested was filmed here. They were going through the loot and realised that some seems to have been stolen by Billy the Fish. They are all arguing and blaming each other so don't notice the police arrive.

Robbery (1967)

Dir. Peter Yates

19-21 Hatton Garden, EC1N 8BA
Dave (William Marlowe), Frank (Barry Foster) and Freddy (Patrick Jordon) are sitting in the stolen ambulance on Hatton Garden as a Vanden Plas Princess passes by. The car then parks outside a jeweller on the junction with Greville Street. Whilst they are inside the building a traffic warden places a device on the car.

53 Queen Victoria Street, EC4N 4SG
As the Jaguar and the ambulance follow the courier, they head down this street with the corner of Friday Street to the left and 53 Queen Victoria Street in the background.

Trafalgar Square, WC2N 5DN
The Vanden Plas Princess drives towards Trafalgar Square, past Charing Cross main station and Admiralty Arch in the distance. From Trafalgar Square they turn into Northumberland Avenue.

Northumberland Avenue (corner of Great Scotland Yard), SW1A 2BD
The timer on the Vanden Plas Princess counts down on this road before releasing a gas which causes the driver to pass out and drive the car into a skip. A local policeman flags down Frank's ambulance and Dave loads the courier into the back.

Trafalgar Square, WC2N 5DN (courtesy of Charlie Forman, Wikimedia Commons)

Wheatley house 1-44 Harbridge Avenue, Roehampton, SW15 4DP
Frank parks the ambulance next to Jack's car in front of a block of flats on Harbridge Avenue. The police on patrol view the ambulance from Danebury Avenue looking towards Harbridge Avenue.

Delamare Terrace, W2 6PF
The radio operator in the police car radios through that they are following the jaguar onto Delamare Terrace, which was filmed from the footbridge over the Grand Union Canal.

The police smash the window of the Jaguar, but the occupants are all able to flee. Gayford House is in the background and the area hasn't changed much in the last 40 or so years.

376-384 Oxford Street, W1C 1JY
The chase takes us around Marble Arch and down Oxford Street, where two motor-cycle cops join them from Bird Street which has the much-loved C & A on the corner. Until recently this was a Gap and is currently being refurbished.

George Eliot Primary School, Marlborough Hill, NW8 0NH
A lollipop man (David Storm) stops traffic outside the school allowing a class of children to cross the road as the Jaguar speeds towards them, and the police car crashes to avoid them.

Victoria Station, Terminus Place, SW1V 1JR
Paul Clifton (Stanley Baker) and his wife Catherine (Joanna Pettet) arrive at Victoria Station, and he puts her into a taxi. Although the station has been extensively reconfigured since this film was made, the forecourt and taxi rank on Terminus Place still has the original cast iron roof.

Grosvenor Gardens, SW1W 0RP
After seeing the note in the newspaper Clifton runs across the road from Terminus Place to Grosvenor Gardens with the statue of Ferdinand Foch prominent in the shot.

Serpentine Bar and Kitchen, Hyde Park, Serpentine Road, W2 2UH
www.benugo.com/sites/restaurants/serpentine-bar-kitchen

Whitely Asset Management Ltd, 116 Princedale Road, W11 4NH

Inspector George Langdon (James Booth) meets with an informant in the Serpentine Restaurant in Hyde Park.

They are open daily for food and drink.

Platform 2, Marylebone Station, NW1 6JJ

Clifton walks along the platform at Marylebone as the night train is being loaded. They think there is up to £4m on board the train. This was shot facing platform two.

Leader's Gardens, Putney Embankment, SW15 1LW

Clifton tells Robinson (Frank Finlay) that he is being watched by a policewoman who is sitting on a bench in the park. The children's playground equipment has changed but the outbuilding is the same although now it is a café called Loo Loo's (Ashlone Road, SW15 1LS).

Leyton Orient, Brisbane Road, E10 5NF

Dave (William Marlowe) and Frank (Barry Foster) go into the stadium through the north terrace entrance to meet with two other gang leaders. Within the terraces Don (Michael McStay) and Ben (George Sewell) meet up as the game carries on in the background.

Bottle Kiln, Walmer Road, W11 4NN

Shortly after the proceeds of the robbery are flown out of the country, there is a news reporter on Walmer Road.

Although the area has been redeveloped since then the chimney known as the Bottle Kiln is still standing. This was used until the middle of the nineteenth century in the local pottery industry and was part of a factory making flowerpots and drainpipes.

Whitely Asset Management Ltd, 116 Princedale Road, W11 4NH

The corner of Hippodrome Place and Pottery Lane was used for the outside of the court. At the time the Earl of Zetland Pub was on the corner of the Princedale Road. This has since closed as a pub and is now an office block but still retains the pub sign.

Sexy Beast (2000)

Dir. Jonathan Glazer

JW Marriott Grosvenor House Hotel, Park Lane, W1K 7TN

This is where Gary Dove (Ray Winstone) stays under the pseudonym of Rowntree. He was convinced to return to London for the bank job by Don Logan (Ben Kingsley).

Clock House, Rutland Mews West, SW7 1NZ

This was Harry's (James Fox) home where he was shot by Teddy Bass (Ian McShane).

The Bank Job (2008)

Dir. Roger Donaldson

59 Queen's Gate Mews, South Kensington, SW7 5QN

This is the address where Martine Love (Saffron Burrows) and Tim Everett (Richard Lintern) go, after she has brought Terry Leather on board for the robbery. The car initially drives around the corner near number 57. They head into number 59.

This street was also used for the handover of credit cards and cash to Gale Benson (Hattie Morahan). If you stand on the corner of Queen's Gate Terrace, the car was parked on the left by the black railings.

RiDa East, 10a Blossom Street, E1 6PL

The external shots of the Denmark Club where Terry first tells his gang about the potential robbery and where Michael X (Peter de Jersey) speaks with Lew Vogel (David Suchet) about 'running his girls' whilst he's away, were filmed here.

Lloyds Bank, 185 Baker Street, NW1 6XB

This was the Lloyd's bank where the photos of Princess Margaret were stored and where the robbery took place.

189 Baker Street, NW1 6UY

This is where the robbers rented the shop 'Le Sac' so they could access the space out the back in order to drill a tunnel into the bank. The building is now an estate agent.

7 Sackville Street, W1S 3DE

This was the location of the tailors where Terry went to speak to Guy Singer (James Faulkner) about being the front buyer for Le Sac.

Aldwych Station, Surrey Street, WC2R 2ND

The scenes shot at Baker Street station as Eddie (Michael Jibson) gets off the tube, as well as the meet-up on Tottenham Court Road for Terry to hand over the pictures, and Edgware Road when Kevin (Stephen Campbell Moore) gets off the tube was filmed at the abandoned Aldwych Station.

ROBBERIES | 59

Above: Aldwych Station, Surrey Street, WC2R 2ND (courtesy of Chris Roberts, Wikimedia Commons)

Right: 8 Endsleigh Gardens, WC1H 0EG

Aldwych Station was officially closed in 1994, as it was not cost effective to renovate it. However, it has been used as a filming location since then and is occasionally opened to the public for specialist tours run by the London Transport Museum.

Montage of police trying to find the right bank:

- Barclays Bank, Goldsmiths' Hall, Foster Lane, EC2V 6BN
- 8 Endsleigh Gardens, WC1H 0EG

Paddington Platform 1, Paddington Station, Praed Street, W2 1HB

- Midlands Bank, Goldsmiths' Hall, Gresham Street, EC2V 7HN
- Lloyds Bank, Wax Chandlers' Hall, 6 Gresham Street, EC2V 7AD

79 Canrobert Street, E2 6PX

Dave Shilling (Daniel Mays) is picked up by Vogel's (David Suchet) men.

Paddington Platform 1, Paddington Station, Praed Street, W2 1HB

Terry sets up a meeting under the clock on platform one with Tim Everett, Lew Vogel, Detective Given and Lord Mountbatten. The newsstand was set up for the movie.

The external shots where Eddie is bundled out of the car and the fight between Terry and Vogel's gang were actually filmed in Chatham's dockyards.

The Italian Job (1969)

Dir. Peter Collinson

HMP Wormwood Scrubs, 160 Du Cane Road, W12 0AN

Charlie Croker (Michael Caine) is released from prison at the start of the film. This was filmed outside Wormwood Scrubs.

The gates are now black but other than that the building is the same.

Royal Lancaster Hotel, Lancaster Terrace, W2 2TY

To celebrate Charlie's freedom his friends throw a party at the Royal Lancaster Hotel. He had a choice of young women to celebrate with.

In 2017, the hotel went through an £80m renovation so the ground floor entrance looks completely different. The mid-century main block of the hotel, however, has remained the same.

18 Denbigh Close, W11 2QH

Charlie lived on Denbigh Close, just off Portobello Road. From the roof of this building, Lorna (Margaret Blye) throws out a girl's belonging after she finds him cheating. The three girls then run out of the flat in their underwear and flee down Denbigh Close.

18 Denbigh Close, W11 2QH

Peninsula Heights, 93 Albert Embankment, SE1 7TY
The robbery is organised in the penthouse at the top of Peninsula Heights. At the time of filming, this building was named Alembic House.

Crystal Palace Park, Thicket Road, SE19 2BA
There is a small patch of grass between Canada Gates and South Terrace Gates where the infamous scene of the white Morris van exploding was filmed. The gang watch on with Charlie Crocker delivering the classic line, 'You're only supposed to blow the bloody doors off!'

Too many explosives were used in the scene and when the van exploded the crew started to make their getaway in case the police were called.

The area has been redeveloped since the 1960s but the road which runs between the gates follows the original racetrack.

Thunderbirds (2004)

Dir. Jonathan Frakes

Jubilee Gardens, Belvedere Road, SE1 7PG
As Thunderbird 2 lands in Jubilee Gardens the news reporter does a piece to camera. It's possible to see Hungerford Bridge and the large Shell Centre white tower block in the background.

Jubilee Gardens, Belvedere Road, SE1 7PG

Riverside Walk, Eye Pier, SE1 7PB
The crowds watch as the Mole tunnels under the Thames. It is possible to see Hungerford Bridge and the Golden Jubilee Bridge from the shot.

Golden Jubilee Bridge, WC2N 6NU
John (Lex Shrapnel), Gordon (Ben Torgersen), Scott (Philip Winchester), Jeff (Bill Paxton) and Virgil (Dominic

UCL, Malet Place, WC1E 6AE (courtesy of Paul Brockenhurst)

Colenso) watch the rescue of the monorail passengers from the northern part of the Golden Jubilee Bridge.

University College Gower Street, WC1E 6BT
The UCL quad and the Wilkins Building stand in for the bank where the Hood (Ben Kingsley) and his gang are carrying out their plan. Alan (Brady Corbet), Fermat (Soren Fulton) and Tintin (Vanessa Hudgens) are able to defeat him. Lady Penelope's pink car was parked just at the foot of the portico steps.

3

MURDER

Murder has been a staple of the crime genre since the very first silent movies, and the first murder mystery was *Sherlock Holmes Baffled* (1900). The sub-genre is so popular that is actually crosses into other genres including gangland films, cosy mysteries, cop dramas, prison films and even courtroom dramas. In this section we have focused on films where murder is the core of the plot, whether that is a whodunnit, revenge or a sub-plot.

The Da Vinci Code (2006)

Dir. Ron Howard

Temple Church, Inner Temple Lane, Temple, EC4Y 7BB
www.templechurch.com

After deciphering the clue 'in London lies a knight a Pope interred. His labour's fruit a Holy wrath incurred. You seek the orb that ought be on his tomb,' Robert Langdon (Tom Hanks) and Sophie Neveu (Audrey Tautou) initially search the effigies at Temple Church for a knight, before realising they are not looking for an effigy but a tomb.

The Church of Inner and Middle Temple was consecrated in 1185 and was the Knights Templar Headquarters. The church is circular and is a replica of the Church of the Holy Sepulchre at Jerusalem. The church is occasionally opened to the public.

Temple Bar Memorial Dragon, WC2R 1DA
Langdon and Neveu leave the Temple Church and are chased by Silas (Paul Bettany) and Remy Jean (Jean-Yves Berteloot). They run down the Strand towards the Temple Bar Memorial Dragon statue. This statue was erected in 1880 and represents the ceremonial entrance to the City of London from Westminster.

Tower Bridge, Tower Bridge Road, SE1 2UP
Remy Jean and Silas drive to the safe house with Leigh Teabing (Ian McKellen) in the boot of their car.

The car is seen driving over Tower Bridge.

207 Gloucester Terrace, W2 6HX
Silas goes to the Opus Dei safe house. The exterior shots were filmed at Gloucester Terrace, which is a private house.

Westminster Abbey, Broad Sanctuary, 20 Deans Yard, SW1P 3PA

It is here that, later in the film Silas accidently shoots his mentor Bishop Manuel Aringarosa (Alfred Molina).

Westminster Abbey, Broad Sanctuary, 20 Deans Yard, SW1P 3PA
After realising they were searching in the wrong church, Langdon decides to go to Westminster Abbey, to look for Sir Isaac Newton's tomb. Later in the movie Teabing is arrested here and taken away by the police, just as he works out the riddle.

All the exterior shots were filmed at Westminster Abbey, but the interior shots were in Lincoln Cathedral.

Wormwood Scrubs, 160 Du Cane Road, W12 0AN

Dr Crippen (1962)

Dir. Robert Lynn

Old Bailey, EC4M 7EH
The trial of Dr Hawley Crippen (Donald Pleasance) was carried out at the Central Criminal Court at the Old Bailey.

HMP Wormwood Scrubs, 160 Du Cane Road, W12 0AN
When found guilty Dr Crippen is imprisoned at Wormwood Scrubs prison. The external wall is now somewhat higher than it was in the 1960s.

Hot Fuzz (2007)

Dir. Edgar Wright

Finchley Nurseries, Burtonhole Lane, NW7 1AS

This is the garden centre where Nicholas Angel (Simon Pegg) chases the killer who murdered Leslie Tiller (Anne Reid) with the garden shears. Angel jumps through the glass window to continue the chase.

Hendon Police Training College, Aerodrome Road, NW9 5JE

The scenes of Nicholas Angel training to be a copper were filmed here.

Kiss Before Dying (1991)

Dir. James Dearden

First National Bank of Chicago, First Chicago House, 90 Long Acre, WC2E 9RA

This was used as the Philadelphia Central Police Headquarters in this film.

Luther: The Fallen Sun (2023)

Dir. Jamie Payne

Old Bailey, EC4M 7EH

John Luther's (Idris Elba) trial was held here and there was lots of press coverage from outside.

Queen Alexandra's House, Bremner Road, Kensington Gore, South Kensington, SW7 2QT

David Robey (Andy Serkis) visits his wife Connie (Hattie Morahan) in her care home here. The Royal Albert Hall can be seen in the background.

63A Brick Lane, E1 6QL

Luther drives down Brick Lane after escaping from prison passing the Eastern Eye Balti House on the left on the corner of Princely Street.

Brace Orthodontist, 15 Artillery Passage, E1 7LJ

Turning right down Parliament Court you will be thrown into the Soho alley where Luther tracks down the transmitter for the murder recording. This alley doesn't have all the sex and peep shows as they were added for the film.

Piccadilly Circus, W1V 9LB

Luther walks down Glasshouse Street, and past Boots towards Piccadilly Circus. Robey threatens a passer-by with a knife with Lilywhites in the background.

Then the three people jump from the surrounding buildings: the first from the Quadrant Arcade building (corner of Regent's Street and Piccadilly); the second from the top of the advertisement screen above Boots; and the third from the top of Lilywhites.

Charing Cross Station, Strand, WC2N 5HF

After the scene at Piccadilly Circus Luther and David Robey run down the stairs to the platform, which is the abandoned Charing Cross Jubilee Line platform.

Old Bailey, EC4M 7EH (courtesy of GrindtXX, Wikimedia Commons)

Aldwych Station, Surrey Street, WC2R 2ND
The fight scene between Luther and Robey continues on the platform at another abandoned station at Aldwych. This is where the young policeman, Jamal (Carl Spencer) was shot and subsequently died.

Aldwych Station was officially closed in 1994, as it was not cost effective to renovate it. However, it has been used as a filming location since then and is occasionally opened to the public for specialist tours run by the London Transport Museum.

Vendetta (2013)

Dir. Stephen Reynolds

Northcote Arms, 110 Grove Green Road, E11 4EL
www.northcotee11.com

Jimmy (Danny Dyer) goes here when he returns to London following the murder of his parents. He questions Terry (Ben Shockley) about what he saw and finds out Terry was the one who had called the fire service but still watched the house burn.

The Northcote Arms is open every day for food and drink but check for specific times.

Rotherhithe Tunnel, 157 Rotherhithe Street, SE16 5QJ
Jimmy drives through here after getting the tip off from the policeman about who killed his parents.

Peacock Gym, 8-9 Caxton Street North, E16 1JL
Jimmy goes to the gym and beats up Warren Evans (Joshua Osei) in the car park and asks for the names of everyone who killed his parents. He then sets fire to the car with Warren in it.

Later he heads to the gym with Ronnie (Nick Nevern) to get some guns to finish his vendetta.

Birkbeck Tavern, 45 Langthorne Road, E11 4HL
www.thebirkbecktavern.co.uk

The Detective, Spencer Holland (Alistair Petrie) went to the pub to get Terry's CCTV footage showing Jimmy putting the body in the back of the car.

The Birkbeck Tavern is open daily for drinks.

Royal Victoria Dock Bridge, 1 Western Gateway, E16 1XL
Holland meets with Dennis (Samuel Kayne) to discuss the murders which have taken place.

Big Moe's Diner, 3 Jenkins Lane, IG11 0AD
Holland meets with Colonel Leach (Vincent Regan), who demands that he hand over everything he knows about Vickers. Leach makes it clear than Vickers is not to be arrested.

Big Moe's Diner closed in 2018.

SERIAL KILLERS

The European film industry differed from the American market and the earliest silent crime films in Europe were about serial killers rather than robberies, and they were in general darker and more psychotic than American movies. It wasn't really until the 1970s and the release of *10 Rillington Place* (1971), and then later *Silence of the Lambs* (1991) that they became popular although there is a tendency to slip over into the slasher movie genre which some consider to be horror rather than crime.

10 Rillington Place (1971)

Dir. Richard Fleischer

Putney Bridge, SW6 3JL
At the end of the movie the policeman spots John Christie (Richard Attenborough) on Putney Bridge before he is arrested.

Last Night in Soho (2021)

Dir. Edgar Wright

Criterion Theatre, 218-223 Piccadilly, St James's, W1J 9HR
www.criterion-theatre.co.uk

The movie starts with a still of Ellie's (Thomasin McKenzie) mum and grandmother in front of the Criterion Theatre in Piccadilly.

The Criterion was opened in 1874 and is one of the few remaining independent theatres in London.

Paddington Station Taxi Rank, Praed Street, W2 1HB
Ellie starts her life in London at Paddington Station, where she walks up the escalator to the taxi rank to pick up a black cab.

University of the Arts, London (UAL), John Princes Street, W1G 0BJ
A number of external shots were taken of UAL, Ellie's university. The interior library shots, however, were filmed in the SOAS library in Russell Square.

Empire Cinemas, 63-65 Haymarket, SW1Y 4RL
The internal shots of Café de Paris, where Eloise first sees her alter-ego Sandy (Anya Taylor-Joy) were filmed at the Empire.

This cinema has permanently closed.

**Paddington Station Taxi Rank,
Praed Street, W2 1HB**

Soho Square, Soho, W1D 3QP
A number of scenes show Ellie walking through Soho Square, including shots where she is walking to and from her job at the Toucan Pub on Carlisle Street.

Old Compton Street, Soho, W1D 5NG
Ellie walks along Old Compton Street and in the background are the bright signs of Slim Chickens.

The Toucan, 19 Carlisle Street, W1D 3BY
www.thetoucansoho.co.uk

Ellie works in The Toucan pub on Carlisle Street. The filming was done both inside and outside the pub.
  The Toucan is an Irish pub which specialises in Guinness and is open every afternoon for drinks but is closed on Sunday.

Percy Passage, Fitzrovia, W1T 1RH
The alleyway leading to Rathbone Street was the location of the scene where Ellie chases after Sandy and is herself being chased by the ghosts from the library. She falls down onto the cold and damp ground, waking up some time later.

Maple Street, Fitzrovia, W1T 4BN
Ellie's student accommodation block is located on Maple Street. This was filmed at the real-life Ramsay Hall residence, which is part of University College London.

8 Goodge Place, W1T 4SG
Sandy/Ellie live in the top floor flat here.
  The black building on the corner was a café in the film, but currently it is a security store.

Carnaby Street, W1F 9PS
As with all 1960s London-based films there is an establishing shot in Carnaby Street.

The Blue Posts, Berwick Street, W1F 0QA
www.theblueposts.net

In one of these establishing shots the Blue Posts pub is visible on Berwick Street.
  They are open every day for drinks.

13 Greek Street, W1D 4DN
As Ellie comes out of the vintage clothes shop, she sees the Rialto logo on a building opposite, alongside signs for Wedgewood Mews and Parkland House.
  The logo was added to a gap in the stonework on 13 Greek Street.

Truman Brewery, 91 Brick Lane, E1 6QR
www.trumanbrewery.com

The final end-of-year fashion show was held in the Truman Brewery on Brick Lane.
  The Truman Brewery is an arts and media centre with a number of

galleries, independent shops, bars and restaurants.

Peeping Tom (1960)

Dir. Michael Powell

Newman Arms, 23 Rathbone Street, W1 1NG
www.thenewmanarms.co.uk

The first of Mark Lewis's victims was picked up just off Oxford Street and taken to her room above the Newman Arms pub where her murder is filmed.

The pub offers food and drink but is closed on Sundays.

8 Melbury Road, W14 8LR
The home footage scenes were filmed in the garden of this house, which was the director's at the time. He appears in the videos as the father.

This was opposite the home of the serial killer, Mark Lewis (Karlheinz Böhm) at number 5 which has since been pulled down and replaced with a block of flats.

Italian Bear Chocolate, 29 Rathbourne Place, W1T 1JG
This is where the elderly gentleman (Miles Malleson) buys a selection of adult photographs as well as the Times and the Guardian. Above the newsagent was Mark Lewis's studio. It is now a chocolate restaurant.

Whitefield School, Claremont Road, Brent Cross, NW2 1AS
This school was built between 1953 and 1954 and was used as the library in *Peeping Tom*.

Tony (2009)

Dir. Gerard Johnson

Ridley Road, E8 2NR
The opening scene shows Tony (Peter Ferdinando) walking through the market on Ridley Road, popping out opposite Dalston Kingsland overground station.

27 Clarissa Street, E8 4HJ
Tony stops to talk about football with a kid on the estate on Clarissa Road. Some of the street has been redeveloped since the film was made but the one-storey blocks with the sloping roof is clearly visible.

Regent Square Gardens, WC1H 8HZ
Tony goes to the phone box on the corner of Regent Square Gardens, to call a woman from one of the cards in the phone box, when he gets pulled out by two lads (Rob Seth-Smith and Neil Large) who want to call their dealer.

Carlton Cinema, 161-169 Essex Road, N1 2TS
Tony and the two lads he met in the phone box, walk past this old cinema,

Regent Square Gardens, WC1H 8HZ

which is derelict in the film. Today it is Gracepoint venue hire.

This used to be the Carlton Cinema, built in 1930 at the height of the Tutankhamun craze hence the Egyptian-style decoration on the facade. It is now Grade II listed but is in quite poor condition.

The Joiner's Arms, 116-118 Hackney Road, E2 7QL

After killing the drug addict Tony heads to the Joiner's Arms gay pub on Hackney Road. It was here he picks up Alex (Lorenzo Camporese) in the toilets after watching him dance.

This pub is now closed and stands empty.

Trafalgar Court, Wapping Wall, E11W 3TF

Tony stands on the semi-circular Thames Path looking out over Canary Wharf, just before he throws three bags of body parts into the Thames.

ESPIONAGE

Espionage films are a popular choice and cover a number of sub-genres from classic literature-based characters such as James Bond, to the spoof 'spook' films like *Johnny English* and *Kingsman*. Modern espionage movies seem to be less about gathering intelligence and more about running around the world (or London in this case) stopping a deranged lunatic from wanting to take over the planet. This idea of a super villain was born out of the Cold War fears of the 1950s when these types of films came into their own.

The Bourne Ultimatum (2007)

Dir. Paul Greengrass

78-83 Hatton Garden, EC1N 8JS

The journalist Simon Ross (Paddy Considine) crosses the road in front of The Guardian Building on Hatton Garden.

This building is a now a co-working space called The Johnson Building.

Waterloo Train Station, Waterloo Road, SE1 8SW

Jason Bourne (Matt Damon) arrives in London on the Eurostar at Waterloo Station. He contacts Simon Ross who meets him at the York Road entrance. Bourne drops a burner phone into Ross's pocket.

Once back on the concourse, Bourne guides Ross via phone in order to identify who is following him. When Bourne identifies one he kills him outside WHSmith.

The director for the film used real CCTV footage from the station in these scenes alongside steady-cam footage to give it a sense of realism.

Charing Cross Underground Station, WC2N 5HF

The subsequent chase into the Underground was filmed on the abandoned Jubilee Line platform at Charing Cross, not Waterloo.

Since the Jubilee Line extension project in 1999, Jubilee Line trains no longer stop at Charing Cross, and along with Aldwych this platform is a favourite with film directors.

Fast and Furious 6 (2013)

Dir. Justin Lin

Lambeth Bridge, Lambeth Road, SE1 7LB

The aftermath of an attack on a Russian military convoy, was filmed on Lambeth Bridge. This included a number of burned-out wrecks as well as one car being removed from a window of 9 Millbank. This is likely created in post-production rather than actually driving a car through the window.

Senate House University of London, Malet Street, WC1E 7HU

The Russian Interpol Headquarters was filmed at Senate House, where Luke Hobbs (Dwayne Johnson) questions a suspect. Both internal and external shots were filmed here.

Cannon Place, 78 Cannon Street, EC4N 6HN

Hobbs assembles his team to discuss the Nightshade Device. This was filmed inside at Cannon Place.

St Lawrence Jewry C of E Church, Guildhall Yard, EC2V 5AA

The crew are involved in a car chase through London. Sniper, Owen Shaw (Luke Edwards) is waiting on the roof of an office block with the clock tower of this church visible behind him.

The church was initially built in 1136 and was destroyed in the Great Fire of London in 1666. Then it was rebuilt by Christopher Wren, only to be damaged in the Blitz. Like a phoenix it has once more been restored.

Old Billingsgate, 1 Old Billingsgate Walk, EC3R 6DX

Hobbs and Tej (Ludacris) are at a motor auction on the terrace of Old Billingsgate. They hope to identify the manufacturer of Shaw's (Luke Evans) custom car. They get into an altercation with the organiser who assumes they are staff and tries to move them on.

This Victorian building was the Billingsgate Fish Market, but now it is a rather swanky events space.

Hare Row, Cambridge Heath, E2 9BY

Dominic Torretto (Vin Diesel) and Brian O'Conner (Paul Walker) look for a Russian shell with an arms dealer. The pawn shop which was the front for his business was filmed on Hare Row, a much quieter street than it appears in the film.

Aldwych Station, Surrey Street, WC2R 2ND

www.ltmuseum.co.uk/hidden-london

Letty (Michelle Rodriguez) and Riley Hicks (Gina Carano) get involved in a fight in an underground station.

The scene was filmed in two locations. The tiled pedestrian walkways were filmed at the long-abandoned Aldwych Station, whereas

ESPIONAGE | 77

Senate House University of London, Malet Street, WC1E 7HU

the shiny modern parts are the new extension at Waterloo Station. See if you can spot the split.

Aldwych Station was officially closed in 1994, as it was not cost effective to renovate it. However, it has been used as a filming location since then and is occasionally opened to the public for specialist tours run by the London Transport Museum.

UK Foreign & Commonwealth Office, King Charles Street, SW1A 2AH

The unlikely location of a pre-street-race party is the UK Foreign & Commonwealth Office. The race itself then starts on King Charles Street through the arch leading to Whitehall.

Whitehall, SW1 2AY

The street race is carried out in Whitehall leading to Piccadilly Circus, along the Embankment to the River.

Battersea Power Station, 188 Kirtling Street, Nine Elms, SW8 5BN

The police chase Torretto and Letty to a piece of waste ground by Battersea Power Station.

At the time of filming the power station was derelict but now is a bustling shopping mall with luxury flats. There is certainly no waste ground, but the iconic shape of the towers is still evident.

Jack Ryan: Shadow Recruit (2014)

Dir. Kenneth Branagh

New Square, Lincoln's Inn, WC2A 3RJ

Jack Ryan (Chris Pine) wakes up in New Square in front of the Treasury office building and realises something important is happening although he's not sure what.

He follows a crowd through the Undercroft of the Lincoln's Inn Chapel and watches a report on a wall-mounted TV about planes flying into the Twin Towers. This is meant to be the London School of Economics building.

The Lincoln's Inn Chapel was designed and built by Inigo Jones in 1623.

London School of Economics, Houghton Street, WC2A 2AE

Also at the London School of Economics (but this time really) Jack watches the events of 9/11 as they unfold.

Building 3 North London Business Park, Oakleigh Road South, N11 1GN

Jack is treated for injuries obtained in Afghanistan in the Walter Reed Military Medical Centre, Washinton DC.

Except it's not Washington. The internal shots are the North London Business Park, in the Virgin Active gym.

53-54 St John's Square, EC1V 4JL

Cathy (Keira Knightley) and Jack have dinner at a fancy Manhattan restaurant, when Ryan is distracted by the news. Cathy is trying to catch him in a lie as she found a cinema ticket in his pocket for *Sorry, Wrong Number*.

This Manhattan restaurant was the Artisan of Clerkenwell. This has since closed and is currently empty.

Victoria House, 37-63 Bloomsbury Square, WC1B 4DA

The Moscow Hotel Grushinsky was closer to home at Victoria House in Bloomsbury.

CGI was used to make it look like it was actually filmed in Russia.

Westminster Cathedral, Victoria Street, SW1P 1LT

Westminster Cathedral was the location of the interior shots of the deserted church where Cherevin (Kenneth Branagh) swears vengeance on America.

Exchange House, Primrose Street, Broadgate, EC2A 2EG

Viktor Cherevin's high rise office block was filmed at Exchange House. Both the internal and external shots were filmed here.

Senate House, Malet Street, WC1E 7HU

Jack takes Cathy to meet Cherevin and this was filmed in the foyer of Senate House.

Victoria House, 37-63 Bloomsbury Square, WC1B 4DA

James Bond Franchise

Sean Connery
Sean Connery held the title of 007 between 1962 and 1971 and starred in six films: *Dr No* (1962), *From Russia with Love* (1963), *Goldfinger* (1964), *Thunderball* (1965), *You Only Live Twice* (1965) and *Diamonds are Forever* (1971).

Dr No (1962)

Dir. Terence Young

Les Ambassadeurs Club, 5 Hamilton Place, W1J 7ED
www.lesambassadeurs.com

Bond is playing cards at Les Ambassadeurs Club. The gaming room was recreated in Pinewood Studios, but the club was and still is in existence. It is advertised as, 'A members only gambling club for the premium player.' Do they come more premium than 007?

Les Ambassadeurs Club at Hamilton Place has been a meeting place of the rich and famous since the Georgian period and was once owned by Leopold de Rothschild (1845-1917). It was reopened in its current form in 1991 and according to the website is 'one of the most exclusive casinos and sought after memberships in the world.'

Goldfinger (1964)

Dir. Guy Hamilton

RAF Northolt, West End Road, Ruislip, HA4 6NG
www.raf.mod.uk/our-organisation/stations/raf-northolt

Blue Grass, Kentucky, Baltimore which housed Pussy Galore's Flying Circus was filmed at RAF Northolt.

As a working air base this isn't open to the public although there is a specialist museum on site. This is accessible by appointment only.

George Lazenby only starred in one movie, *On Her Majesty's Secret Service* (1969).

On Her Majesty's Secret Service (1969)

Dir. Peter R. Hunt

College of Arms, 130 Queen Victoria Street, EC4V 4BT
www.college-of-arms.gov.uk

Bond needed to pass himself off as Sir Hilary Bray (George Baker) and therefore took a crash course at the College of Arms which is the official heraldic authority for the UK and the Commonwealth. It was founded in 1484 and has the responsibility for issuing coats of arms, registers of arms, pedigrees, genealogies, and changes of name and flags.

At the start of this movie, Lazenby acknowledges Sean Connery when lying on a Portuguese beach. He says: 'This never happened to the other fella'.

Roger Moore took over the role of Bond between 1973 and 1985 and appeared in seven movies: *Live and Let Die* (1973), *The Man with the Golden Gun* (1974), *The Spy Who Loved Me* (1977), *Moonraker* (1979), *For your Eyes Only* (1981), *Octopussy* (1983) and *A View to a Kill* (1985).

For Your Eyes Only (1981)

Dir. John Glen

Ministry of Defence, Whitehall Court, SW1A 2HB

The exterior shots of the Ministry of Defence were actually filmed at the real Ministry building.

The building was designed by E. Vincent Harris in 1915 but wasn't completed until 1959. It was originally the Headquarters for the Air Ministry and Board of Trade before the Ministry of Defence took over in 1964.

In 2007, a law was passed under the Serious Organised Crime and Police Act 2005 which means that it is illegal to enter this building, scale walls or enter vehicle ramps. Be aware.

Octopussy (1983)

Dir. John Glen

RAF Northolt, West End Road, Ruislip, HA4 6NG

www.raf.mod.uk/our-organisation/stations/raf-northolt

The horse trials attended by the Latin American dictators at a Cuban air base were filmed here at the RAF Northolt Aerodrome.

As a working air base this isn't open to the public although there is a specialist museum on site. This is accessible by appointment only.

Old Royal Naval College, King William Walk, Greenwich, SE10 9NN

www.ornc.org

The Russian National Fine Art Repository, accessed via the Undercroft was filmed at the chapel in the Old Royal Naval College in Greenwich. General Orlov (Steven Berkoff) was called to the Art Repository as 007 had stolen the reproduction of the Fabergé egg.

You can see the towers from Greenwich Power Station in the background of the shot. The chapel and the Painted Hall are open to the public but it is advisable to book in advance.

Sotheby's, 34-35 New Bond Street, W1A 2RP

Old War Office Building, Horse Guards Avenue, SW1A 2EU

The MI6 headquarters in *Octopussy* (1983), *A View to a Kill* (1985), and *Licence to Kill* (1989) was filmed at the Old War Office Building.

The building was completed in 1906 and was the War Office until 1964. The Ministry of Defence continued to occupy the building until 2013. Then it was sold and redeveloped as a Raffles Hotel with 125 rooms or suites, 9 restaurants and bars and a spa. Bond would have approved.

Sotheby's, 34-35 New Bond Street, W1A 2RP

www.sothebys.com/en

The Fabergé egg was put up for auction at Sotheby's by an anonymous seller listed as 'the property of a lady'.

Exterior shots were used when Bond spots the winner of the auction Kamal Khan (Louis Jourdan), leaving with the prized egg.

Timothy Dalton

In 1987, Timothy Dalton took over as Bond and made two films: *The Living Daylights* (1987) and *Licence to Kill* (1989).

The Living Daylights (1987)

Dir. John Glen

Malaysia House, 57 Trafalgar Square, WC2N 5DU

Malaysia House, 57 Trafalgar Square, WC2N 5DU

The exterior shots of MI6 headquarters were filmed at Malaysia House. A sign above the door read 'Universal Exports Ltd' which Fleming used in the original books as a cover for MI6.

Malaysia House originally housed the Malaysian High Commission, which moved in the 1960s to Belgrave Square.

Pierce Brosnan

Pierce Brosnan played Bond in four movies between 1995 and 2002: *Goldeneye* (1995), *Tomorrow Never Dies* (1997), *The World is Not Enough* (1999) and *Die Another Day* (2002).

The World is Not Enough (1999)

Dir. Michael Apted

Vauxhall Cross (SIS Building), 85 Albert Embankment, SE11 5AW

The opening sequence is a boat chase on the Thames starting with the SIS Building at the start. Special effects produce a hole blasted into the side of it.

Vauxhall Cross is the headquarters of the Secret Intelligence Service (SIS) or MI6 and was built in 1994. It was influenced by 1930s modernist architecture.

Glengall Bridge, Millwall Inner Dock, Isle of Dogs, E14 9QY

Bond races through Glengall Bridge as it was closing with all the tension we would expect.

The bridge, built in 1990, is created in the Dutch style after the Langlois Bridge in Arles.

Royal Victoria Dock, Canning Town, E16 3BT

Bond's prototype Q-boat rolls over at Royal Victoria Dock in the chase between Giulietta da Vinci and the Cigar Girl.

The dock was opened in 1855 and was the first royal dock and the first London dock capable of accommodating large steam vessels.

Ornamental Canal, Wapping Lane, Tobacco Dock, E1W 2JX

The traffic wardens get soaked at the right-angle bend of the Ornamental Canal at Discovery Walk. Bond's Q-boat then miraculously bounces up some steps into the 'London Canoe Club'. This was a set. He then ran aground 35 miles away in Chatham, Kent.

Millennium Dome/O2 Arena, Peninsula Square, SE10 0DX

Bond ends the boat chase hanging off the side of the Millennium Dome. At the time of filming the dome was still being constructed.

The Dome was built to commemorate the millennium and was rather controversial as it cost more than £28 million to complete and was intended to be a temporary structure. It was rebranded in 2005 as the O2 Arena and home to various gigs and exhibitions.

RAF Northolt, West End Road, Ruislip, HA4 6NG

www.raf.mod.uk/our-organisation/stations/raf-northolt

The RAF Northolt site in *The World is Not Enough* was used as the Azerbaijani air base.

As a working air base this isn't open to the public although there is a specialist museum on site. This is accessible by appointment only.

Die Another Day (2002)

Dir. Lee Tamahori

The Reform Club, 104 Pall Mall, SW1Y 5EW
www.reformclub.com

Some scenes at the gentleman's club Blades, was filmed at the Reform Club, such as the scene when Bond is given M's calling card – a key which opened the secret door reached by Westminster Bridge. This was filmed in the central lobby, and then later the fencing duel was also filmed there.

The Reform Club was founded in 1836 for those who supported the Great Reform Act (1832). It was a private members' club, and in 1838 they employed a celebrity chef, Alexis Soyer. Their members include Winston Churchill, Arthur Conan Doyle and Camilla, when she was duchess of Cornwall. The Reform Club was the first private members' club to open its doors to women, in 1981.

Buckingham Palace, SW1A 1AA
www.rct.uk/visit/buckingham-palace

Buckingham Palace was used for the dramatic arrival by parachute of the super villain Gustav Grave (Toby Stevens).

The palace is open to the public at certain times of the year but you must book in advance.

Westminster Bridge Road, SE1 7GA

Beneath the Coade Stone lion on the Lambeth side of Westminster Bridge is the secret entrance to the fictional Vauxhall Cross tube station.

These lions are created using mould-fired pottery, known as Coade Stone, rather than stone and have stood guard on the bridge for 160 years.

In a publicity shot for *On Her Majesty's Secret Service*, George Lazenby is caught posing here with Big Ben in the background.

Westminster Bridge Road, SE1 7GA

GoldenEye (1995)

Dir. Martin Campbell

Vauxhall Cross (SIS Building), 85 Albert Embankment, SE11 5AW
The exterior shots of MI6 headquarters and the location of M's (Judi Dench) office were filmed here.

Vauxhall Cross is the headquarters of the Secret Intelligence Service (SIS) or MI6 and was built in 1994. It was influenced by 1930s modernist architecture.

Somerset House, Strand, WC2R 1LA
www.somersethouse.org.uk

The courtyard of Somerset House represented St Petersburg Square where Jack Wade (Joe Don Baker) takes a sledgehammer to his blue Moskovich after picking up Bond from the airport.

Somerset House holds a number of events and exhibitions throughout the year as a working arts centre.

Built in 1779, the North Wing, housed the Royal Academy of Arts and the South Wing completed in 1786, housed the Navy Board. It was also the home of the registry of births, deaths and marriages.

The Langham Hilton, 1c Portland Place, W1B 1JA
www.langhamhotels.com

The scenes of the Grand Hotel Europe which was covered in Russian, British

Somerset House, Strand, WC2R 1LA (courtesy of Emperorzurg123, Wikimedia Commons)

and American flags were filmed here. This was where Bond met with Janus to talk about the helicopter.

This hotel was the first Grand Hotel in Europe and opened in 1865. It had numerous glamorous guests including Louis Napoléon III of France in 1871.

St Pancras Station, Euston Road, N1C 4QP

Platform Five at St Pancras was a stand in for the St Petersburg terminus and Natalya (Izabella Scorupco) alights from an old British Rail train.

Brompton Cemetery, Old Brompton Road, SW5 9JE

The exterior shots of the St Petersburg Church where Natalya hides, were filmed at the rear of the chapel at Brompton Cemetery – on the Fulham Road side.

St Sophia's Greek Cathedral, Moscow Road, Bayswater, W2 4LQ
www.stsophia.org.uk

The interior shots of the St Petersburg's Church where Natalya speaks with Boris (Alan Cumming) were filmed in St Sophia's Greek Cathedral.

The cathedral was built between 1877 and 1899 and designed by John Oldrid Scott. When it was built it was a church but was elevated to cathedral in 1922. It currently has a museum telling the history of the church, although it is open by appointment only.

Drapers' Hall, Throgmorton Street, EC2N 2DQ
www.thedrapers.co.uk

The Drapers' Hall was used for a stand in for the interior shots of St Petersburg's council chamber. This was where General Ouromov (Gottfried John) delivers the report about the Golden Eye detonation.

There has been a building on the Draper's Hall site since the 16th century although it was only bought by the Draper's Guild from Henry VIII in 1543. It was the home of Thomas Cromwell, and ownership transferred to Henry VIII upon his execution in 1540. It was damaged by the Great Fire in 1666 and was rebuilt between 1667 and 1671. Fire ravaged it once more in 1770. The current building dates from 1772 and it was further added to in the 19th century. Tours can be arranged to the site, although it is not generally open to the public.

Tomorrow Never Dies (1997)

Dir. Roger Spottiswoode

Somerset House, Strand, WC2R 1LA
www.somersethouse.org.uk

The Ministry of Defence exterior scenes were filmed at Somerset House.

Somerset House holds a number of events and exhibitions throughout the year as a working arts centre.

Built in 1779, the North Wing, housed the Royal Academy of Arts and the South Wing completed in 1786, housed the Navy Board. It was also the home of the registry of births, deaths and marriages.

Brent Cross Shopping Centre, Prince Charles Drive, NW4 3FP
If you head to level four of the car park at Brent Cross, you will find the location where James Bond escapes from a remote controlled BMW750 – even though it was in reality a 740.

When filming the stunts there was more smoke created than anticipated and the local fire brigade was called.

Daniel Craig
Daniel Craig took the role of James Bond in 2006 and made five films before he ended his run in 2021: *Casino Royale* (2006), *Quantum of Solace* (2008), *Skyfall* (2012), *Spectre* (2015) and *No Time to Die* (2021). He also made a short film as Bond called *Happy and Glorious* (2012) for the opening of the 2012 Olympics in London.

Quantum of Solace (2008)

Dir. Marc Forster

Water Gardens, Edgware Road, W2 2DB
Bond drives to the entrance of the Water Gardens via a concrete underpass. The block is owned by a deceased double agent. It is whilst they are here that he and M (Judi Dench) fully comprehend the power the Quantum organisation has.

The Reform Club, 104 Pall Mall, SW1Y 5EW
www.reformclub.com

M explains Bond's appalling behaviour to a government minister whilst in a government office which was filmed at the Reform Club.

The Reform Club was founded in 1836 for those who supported the Great Reform Act (1832). It was a private members' club, and in 1838 they employed a celebrity chef, Alexis Soyer. Their members include Winston Churchill, Arthur Conan Doyle and Camilla, when she was duchess of Cornwall. The Reform Club was the first private members' club to open its doors to women, in 1981.

Barbican Centre, Upper Frobisher Crescent, Silk Street, EC2Y 8HD
www.barbican.org.uk

The MI6 headquarters was located at the Barbican Centre with some internal shots taken on the third floor on Upper Frobisher Crescent, giving the appearance of an enclosed space. The external shots were filmed in the courtyard facing the crescent.

The Barbican Centre was the epitome of industrial brutalist architecture when it opened in 1982. The Barbican offers

ESPIONAGE | 89

The Reform Club, 104 Pall Mall, SW1Y 5EW (courtesy of Philafrenzy, Wikimedia Commons)

Barbican Centre, Upper Frobisher Crescent, Silk Street, EC2Y 8HD

tours of the centre as well as a range of other events. If you want to channel your inner Bond there is also a Martini bar where you can order it 'shaken, not stirred'.

Skyfall (2012)

Dir. Sam Mendes

National Gallery, Trafalgar Square, WC2N 5DN (Room 34)
www.nationalgallery.org.uk

Bond meets the new Q (Ben Wishaw) at the National Gallery in front of Turner's *The Fighting Temeraire* which is located in room 34.

82 Cadogan Square, SW1X 0EA
M's flat was filmed in Cadogan Square and is where Bond confronts her even though they all think he is dead.
   This flat belonged to John Barry, who composed much of the earlier Bond music and is shown conducting an orchestra at the end of *The Living Daylights*.

Four Seasons Hotel, 10 Trinity Square, EC3N 4AJ
M (Judi Dench) gives evidence to the prime minister's panel at the Four Seasons Hotel.
   This hotel was previously the Port of London Authority Building and was built in 1922 by Sir Edwin Cooper. They were at the site until 1971.

Vauxhall Cross (SIS Building), 85 Albert Embankment, SE11 5AW
The Secret Intelligence Service (SIS) or MI6 exterior shots were filmed at Vauxhall Cross.
   Vauxhall Cross is the headquarters of the Secret Intelligence Service (SIS) or MI6 and was built in 1994. It was influenced by 1930s modernist architecture.

Broadgate Tower, 201 Bishopsgate, EC2M 3AB
The 'Shanghai' high-rise office block was actually Broadgate Tower.

The Vaults, Leake Street, SE1 7NN
www.thevaults.london/leake-street

Bond undertook his fitness evaluation, following the explosion, in The Vaults which was formerly known as the Old Vic Tunnels.
   The Vaults is an art centre for immersive theatre and alternative art.

Westminster Station, SW1A 2NE
Bond leaves Westminster Underground station at the Parliament Street entrance. He heads up Whitehall to save M.
   Bear in mind that Westminster station is normally incredibly busy with tourist traffic so time your visit early in the morning or later in the evening.

1 Whitehall Place, SW1A 2HE
Silva emerges from Embankment Station after the bomb was detonated.

The entrance however was the rear of 1 Whitehall Place near the bin store and was created as a set by the film crew.

Spectre (2015)

Dir. Sam Mendes

Treasury Building, Great George Street, SW1P 3JX
The exterior shots of MI6 headquarters were filmed in the circular courtyard with various aerial shots of people walking across it to enter the various buildings.

1 Stanley Gardens, Notting Hill, W11 2ND
The long shot of Bond's flat was filmed here. If you stand opposite look up to the first floor at the balconette. This was where he was standing looking out of the window.

Camelford House, 89 Albert Embankment, SE1 7TP
The boat ride taking Bond to Q's headquarters takes a scenic route along the Thames including past Camelford House, and the MI5 building (85 Albert Embankment) which exploded at the end of *Skyfall*.

Rules Restaurant, 34-35 Maiden Lane, Covent Garden, WC2E 7LB
Moneypenny (Naomie Harris) and Q are filling M (Ralph Fiennes) in on the whereabouts of Bond, whilst dining at this restaurant. M tells

1 Stanley Gardens, Notting Hill, W11 2ND

them that C (Andrew Scott) has access to the Smart Blood Files and was not to be trusted. Deleting the files meant they wouldn't know where Bond was.

Castle Baynard Tunnel, Castle Baynard Street, EC4V 4EA
Bond's car crashes with Spectre's henchmen at the junction of Castle Baynard Tunnel not far from St Benet Metropolitan Welsh Church.

Rules Restaurant, 34-35 Maiden Lane, Covent Garden, WC2E 7LB

7 Spring Gardens, SW1 2BU

Westminster Bridge, SE1 7GA

Bond shoots down Ernst Stavro Blofeld's (Christoph Waltz) helicopter onto Westminster Bridge with the Houses of Parliament and Big Ben in the background.

Horse Guards Avenue, SW1A 2HU

Bond goes to meet Q to collect the Aston Martin DBS. He heads down Horse Guards Avenue and the statue of Spencer Compton, the 8th Duke of Devonshire, can be seen in the foreground.

7 Spring Gardens, SW1 2BU

Dr Madeleine Swann (Léa Seydoux) tells Bond that she won't stay with him whilst standing in Spring Gardens. The National Gallery and Nelson's column are visible in the background.

Whitehall, SW1A 2AY

The final shot in *Spectre* is an establishing shot in Whitehall facing the statue of Prince George, the Duke of Cambridge. The statue was completed in 1907 using 45 tonnes of granite.

Jason Bourne (2016)

Dir. Paul Greengrass

Woolwich Arsenal Station, Woolwich New Road, SE18 6EU

After Nicky (Julia Stiles) is shot, Jason Bourne (Matt Damon) tries to access her locked memory stick. He starts by travelling from Athens to Berlin. Athens station was actually Woolwich Arsenal.

Sonic Digital, 71 Praed Street, Tyburnia, W2 1NS

Bourne visits former agent, Malcolm Smith (Bill Camp), who is working for a private security firm, stopping to pick up some tech at Sonic Digital first.

Paddington Basin, North Wharf Road, W2 1LF

There are various sequences shot in Paddington Basin, where Jason Bourne and Malcolm Smith (Bill Camp) are being tracked by a number of agents.

Sonic Digital, 71 Praed Street, Tyburnia, W2 1NS

Above: *Fan Bridge, Paddington Basin, North Wharf Road, W2 1LF*

Left: *Brewdog, Harbet Road, W2 1AJ*

They film throughout the Basin, but on the BrewDog patio, Smith waits as Bourne sets off an alarm which results in all the surrounding buildings evacuating.

At 2 Kingdom Street, W2 6BD Bourne sees Smith working in an office block.

Fantasia Grill House, 28 Praed Street, W2 1NH

Robert Dewey (Tommy Lee Jones) intends to kill Bourne so Heather Lee (Alicia Vikander) goes to rescue him. Bourne however, hijacks her van on Praed Street in front of the Fantasia Grill House.

Fantasia Grill House, 28 Praed Street, W2 1NH

Johnny English (2003)

Dir. Peter Howitt

8 John Adam Street, WC2N 6EZ
The external shots of 10 Downing Street were filmed here for the scene where the prime minister is told that only one agent has survived.

This is currently a fire exit for the RSA building, and certain props were added to make the façade look just like the real Number 10.

Maughan Library, Chancery Lane, WC2A 1LR
Johnny English (Rowan Atkinson) and Angus Bough (Ben Miller) travel to the Tower of London to discuss Agent One's investigation of the plot to steal the crown jewels. They watched on as the jewels were stolen. The external shots were filmed at Maughan Library.

Freemasons' Hall, 60 Great Queen Street, WC2B 5AZ
English and Bough are called to the MI7 headquarters, filmed at Freemasons' Hall, to discuss what happened with the crown jewels.

Abingdon Street Car Park, Great College Street, SW1P 3RX
English and Bough leave the Houses of Parliament via the Abingdon Street Car Park, after being tasked with finding the crown jewels.

The Grapes, 14 Lime Street, EC3M 7AN
The hearse escapes through the streets of London and is seen driving past The Grapes Pub.

The pub is open Monday to Friday for food and drink but is closed at weekends.

Leadenhall Market, Gracechurch Street, EC3V 1LT
English and Bough chase the hearse into Leadenhall Market.

Lindsey Street, Barbican, EC1A 9EJ
They continue the chase of the hearse through the streets of Clerkenwell, where it nearly crashes through a group of nuns on the junction with Long Lane.

8 West Smithfield, EC1A 9JR
English spins the car around to continue the pursuit in front of the Ferraris Snack Bar on West Smithfield.

Brompton Cemetery North Lodge, Lillie Road, SW5 9JE
The hearse followed by English ends up at the old Brompton Cemetery, where they disturb a funeral which was taken place. English walks down the steps from one of chapels in the domed area near the chapel, near the Fulham Road end of the cemetery and tries to arrest the attendees of the funeral.

1 Canada Square, E14 5DY
The crown jewels were brought to this building as part of Pascal Edward

ESPIONAGE | 97

Leadenhall Market, Gracechurch Street, EC3V 1LT

3A/B Belvedere Road, SE1 7GP

Sauvage's (John Malcovich) plan to take over the throne of England.

English and Bough plan to parachute down to the headquarters building. However, he lands in the wrong building and then has to enter the right building on foot.

Temple Church, Temple, EC4Y 7BB
The Archbishop of Canterbury (Oliver Ford Davies) is seen leaving this church. Sauvage plans to replace the archbishop for the coronation. The shot was taken at the Pump Court end of the church.

The Church of Inner and Middle Temple was consecrated in 1185 and was the Knights Templar Headquarters. The church is circular and is a replica of the Church of the Holy Sepulchre at Jerusalem. The church is occasionally opened to the public.

3A/B Belvedere Road, SE1 7GP
English finally catches up with Lorna Campbell (Natalie Imbruglia) in a sushi bar and tries to find out more about her.

This was a Yo! Sushi at the time of filming but now it is a Subway.

Wood Street Police Station, 37 Wood Street, Barbican, EC2P 2NQ
Dieter Klein (Steve Nicolson) returned the crown jewels to the police, at Wood Street Police Station, just before Sauvage's coronation.

This police station at the time of writing has been permanently closed down.

Smithfield Market, Grand Avenue, EC1A 9PS
There is an establishing shot of the British people preparing for the coronation and posters of the new 'king'.

Buckingham Palace, SW1A 1AA
When English overcomes Sauvage and foils his plot, he is crowned accidentally in his place. He is then invited to Buckingham Palace to receive a knighthood for the work he had done for the nation.

Buckingham Palace, SW1 1AA (courtesy of Diego Delso, Wikimedia Commons)

Johnny English Strikes Again (2018)

Dir. David Kerr

Lambeth Bridge, Lambeth Road, SE1 7LB

Just after Johnny English (Rowan Atkinson) received his letter, a car is seen driving over Lambeth Bridge, to the north side.

King Charles Street Arch, 100 Parliament Street, SW1A 2NH

The car then drives through King Charles Street arch into the Foreign Commonwealth and Development Office (SW1A 2NH), a building on the right which is meant to be the MI7 building.

Lothbury, EC2R 7HH

When he had broken free of the virtual reality machine, Johnny wanders out of the building onto Lothbury.

Waterstones, 1-3 Whittington Avenue, EC3V 1PJ

When Johnny English is taking part in the virtual reality experience he runs through Waterstones and attacks a number of people he believes to be threats.

41 Bartholomew Lane, EC2N 2AX

He then crawls on his hands and knees over a zebra crossing, which seems to have been added for the film.

60 Threadneedle Street, EC2R 8HP

English then enters a café on Threadneedle Street which was, at the time of filming, part of the Euphorium chain. Now it is the Soho Coffee Co. Here he pushes the old lady in the wheelchair through the door and attacks a member of staff with baguettes.

Kingsman: The Secret Service (2014)

Dir. Matthew Vaughn

Alexandra and Ainsworth Estate, Rowley Way, Camden, NW8 0SN

This is the council estate where Eggsy (Taron Egerton) lives and is first introduced to Harry Hart (Colin Firth) following the death of his father in Afghanistan.

Huntsman, 11 Savile Row, W1S 3PG

This is the Kingsman headquarters which is accessed via the shopfront of number 11 Savile Row. This is Huntsman and Sons bespoke tailor.

Black Prince, 6 Black Prince Road, Kennington, SE11 6HS

www.theblackprincepub.co.uk

Eggsy and his friends go to the pub and steal the keys of the guy they had an argument with and proceeds to do donuts outside the pub to mock him.

Throughout the film this is where all the pub scenes are shot, including the classic one where Harry Hart takes out all five members of the gang who tried to start a fight with Eggsy.

This pub is opened daily for food and drink.

Corbridge Crescent, Cambridge Heath, E2 9EZ

After Eggsy and his friends drive off in the stolen car, they have a backwards car chase with the police, and they drive through a railway bridge and end up smashing into a parked car on Corbridge Crescent.

Holborn Police Station, 15 Lamb's Conduit Street, WC1N 3NR

Following the car chase, Eggsy was arrested and taken to the police station. The external shots were taken at Holborn Police Station. Here he makes the call to the Kingsmen to get him out of trouble.

Imperial College, Prince Consort Road, South Kensington, SW7 2BH

Professor Arnold (Mark Hamill) enters the college through the Royal School of Mines entrance where Harry confronts him just before he explodes. The building was not damaged in the explosion as it was all CGI.

11 Stanhope Mews South, Kensington, SW7 4TF

Harry Hart lives in a house on Stanhope Mews, where his office is decorated with front page headlines from *The Sun*.

Lock & Co., 6 St James's Street, SW1A 1EF

When at Savile Row to get his bespoke suit made, Richmond Valentine (Samuel L. Jackson) was also there and Hart recommends that a hat is needed for Ascot and recommends Lock & Co.

Lock & Co. is the oldest shop in London and the oldest hat shop in the world. It opened in 1676 and every hat is hand made.

Kingsman: The Golden Circle (2017)

Dir. Matthew Vaughn

Huntsman, 11 Savile Row, W1S 3PG

The film opens with Eggsy (Taron Egerton) coming out of the Kingsman

Holborn Police Station, 15 Lamb's Conduit Street, WC1N 3NR

headquarters to be confronted by Charlie Hesketh (Edward Holcroft) and a rather eventful taxi ride.

Florence Nightingale Statue, St James, SW1Y 4AR

The taxi ride finishes here with Charlie being thrown out of the window losing his bionic arm in the process.

Marble Arch, W2 2UH

Eggsy, driving the taxi to escape the people chasing him barges through the gates on Marble Arch into Hyde Park.

Marble Arch, W2 2UH

Serpentine Bar and Kitchen, Hyde Park, Serpentine Road, W2 2UH

www.benugo.com/sites/restaurants/serpentine-bar-kitchen/

Eggsy drives the cab into the Serpentine in front of the Serpentine Bar and Kitchen.

They are open daily for food and drink.

11 Stanhope Mews South, Kensington, SW7 4TF

Eggsy lives in Harry Hart's old house on Stanhope Mews, with his girlfriend

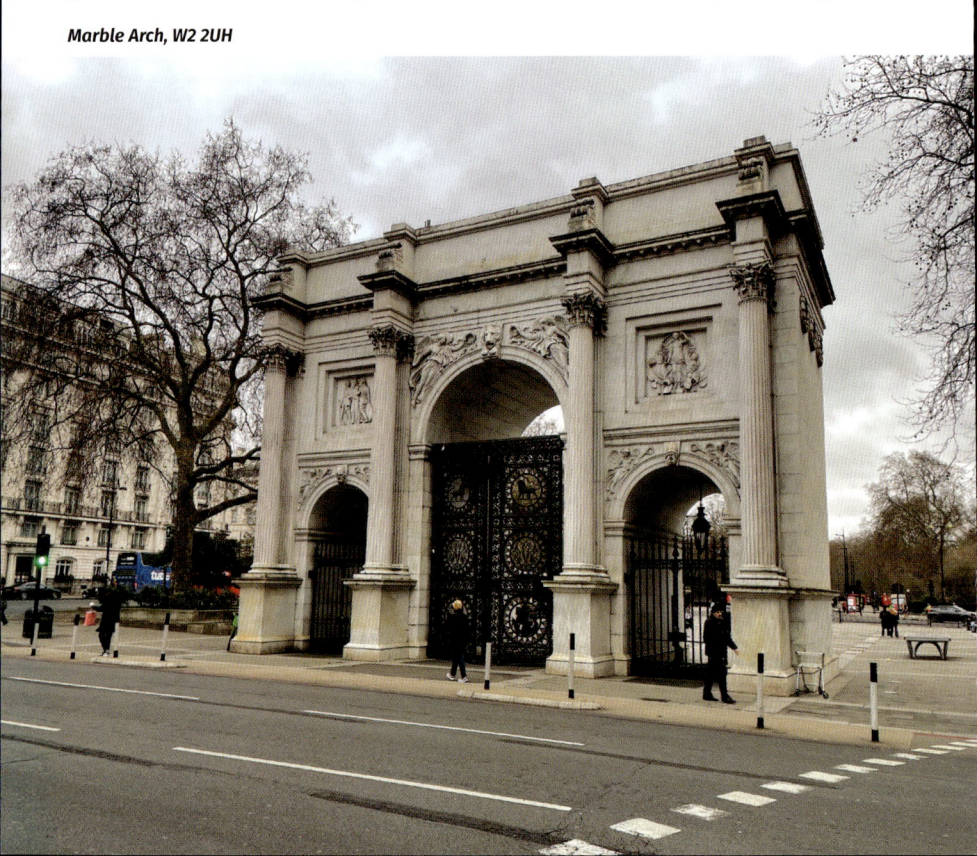

Princess Tilde (Hanna Alström). He has replaced all *The Sun* headlines with three of his own.

Alexandra and Ainsworth Estate, Rowley Way, Camden, NW8 0SN

This is the council estate where Eggsy lived. He meets with his friends here with Tilde before he meets her parents.

Berry Brothers and Rudd, 3 St James's Street, SW1A 1EF

Eggsy and Merlin (Mark Strong) had to find new headquarters for the Kingsman after the old one was hit with a missile.

Hammersmith Apollo, 45 Queen Caroline Street, W6 9QH

The interior of 'Poppy's Amphitheater' where the kidnapped Elton John is forced to play the piano was shot at the Hammersmith Apollo.

Great George Street, SW1P 3AA

Clara (Poppy Anela Delevingne) uses the phone box here, with Big Ben in the background to speak to her boyfriend Charlie who agrees to meet her with the antidote.

Chapel, Old Royal Naval College, SE10 9NN

After saving the world again, Eggsy and Tilde get married in the Chapel at the Old Royal Naval College.

Men in Black International (2019)

Dir. F. Gary Gray

Canary Wharf Station, E14 5LL

Molly (Tessa Thompson) arrives in London from New York on the Jubilee Line alighting at Canary Wharf to be met by High T (Liam Neeson). If only the Underground really was international!

The Reform Club, 104 Pall Mall, SW1Y 5EW

www.reformclub.com

Agent H (Chris Hemsworth) is confronted with a bunch of troublesome aliens at the Reform Club.

The Reform Club was founded in 1836 for those who supported the Great Reform Act (1832). It was a private members' club, and in 1838 they employed a celebrity chef, Alexis Soyer. Their members include Winston Churchill, Arthur Conan Doyle and Camilla, when she was duchess of Cornwall. The Reform Club was the first private members' club to open its doors to women, in 1981.

The Blackfriar, 174 Queen Victoria Street, EC4V 4EG

www.nicholsonspubs.co.uk/restaurants/london/theblackfriarblackfriarslondon

H enters the London MIB HQ via the typewriter shop, although in reality this is actually a pub.

The Blackfriar was built in 1875 on the site of a Dominican Priory. It was then re-designed by H. Fuller-Clark and Henry Poole in 1905 and Poole's original carved friars are still scattered around the bar.

They are open daily for food and drink, and show all major sport fixtures.

Jamie's Ludgate Hill, 47 Ludgate Hill, EC4M 7JZ

H entertains Vungus (Kayvan Novak) at Jamie's. The entrance to the pub was on Ludgate Square in the film, and appears to lead to a bar beneath Jamie's.

The Vault, 1 Old Billingsgate Walk (Riverside, 16 Lower Thames St), EC3R 6DX

The internal shots of the dance club were filmed at Old Billingsgate which is an events hire business. In the basement of the building The Vault has retained the amazing Victorian arches.

Moorfields, EC2Y 9AL

H, M (Tessa Thompson) and Pawny (Kumail Nanjiani) drive out of the MIB underground carpark in pursuit of the agency mole. This was filmed near the British Red Cross office on Moorfields.

Mission: Impossible (1996)

Dir. Brian De Palma

County Hall Building, Belvedere Road, SE1 7PB

The interior shots of the CIA Building in Virginia were filmed in the County Hall Building.

The exterior shots however were filmed in Virginia.

County Hall was opened in 1922, as the headquarters of London County Council, the GLC (Greater London Council) and ILEA (Inner London Education Authority).

Once these entities were disbanded County Hall became an exhibition space and a hotel.

Liverpool Street Underground Station, Liverpool Street, EC2M 1QT

Ethan Hunt's (Tom Cruise) London safe house was located above the Broad Street/Liverpool Street entrance to Liverpool Street Station.

Ethan Hunt is also filmed walking through the main concourse of the station when he has to call Jim Phelps (Jon Voight) to arrange to meet him in Ponti's café.

Anchor Tavern, 34 Park Street, SE1 9EF

Ethan relaxes on the terrace of the Anchor Tavern with Luther Stickell (Ving Rhames).

The Anchor was built in 1615, and boasts Samuel Pepys watching the Great Fire of London on the north side of the river from here in 1666.

Mission Impossible: Rogue Nation (2015)

Dir. Christopher McQuarrie

Piccadilly Circus Underground Station, W1B 5DQ

Ethan Hunt (Tom Cruise) exits Piccadilly Circus tube station at the Regent's Street exit. He runs up Regent Street to a record shop for his briefing.

5 Air Street, W1J 0AD

The record shop was filmed on Air Street. The interior of the shop with the listening booths was a set.

Currently this store is Hawksmoor Steak House, and although they don't have listening booths, you could get a steak.

Great Windmill Street, W1D 7LA

Ethan escapes from the dungeon and makes a call to the IMF organisation from a call box on Great Windmill Street.

Lee Navigation Canal, Three Mill Lane, E3 3DU

Ethan and Benji Dunn (Simon Pegg) get a barge on the Lee Navigation Canal. The mooring is located by Three Mill Lane.

Brompton Cemetery, 5 Adrian Mews, SW10 9AE

Ilsa (Rebecca Ferguson) meets with Solomon Lane (Sean Harris) in Brompton Cemetery after returning to undercover work.

The Farmiloe Building, 34-36 St John Street, EC1 4AZ

The IMF team meet in a warehouse, filmed in the upper floor of the Farmiloe Building. This building isn't open to the public.

St John Street, EC1 4AZ

Brandt (Jeremy Renner) phones Alan Hunley (Alec Baldwin) from a phone box which was set up for the shot on St John Street.

Tower of London, EC3N 4AB

Benji's return is revealed at a restaurant laid out on the cobbles in front of the Tower of London.

The Farmiloe Building, 34-36 St John Street, EC1 4AZ

Tower of London, EC3N 4AB

Elm Court, Middle Temple, EC4Y 7AH

There is no restaurant here, and is an open space thronged with tourists wanting a glimpse of the Tower of London.

Bell Yard, WC2A 2JR
Soloman Lane chases Isla and Ethan through Bell Yard, where they emerge onto the Strand.

Elm Court, Middle Temple, EC4Y 7AH
Ethan and Isla are then chased through Middle Temple. Ethan leaps through a window by the steps on the south east corner of Elm Court.

At the same time Isla has a knife fight with Janik Vinter (Jens Hultén) in the cloisters near Temple Church.

Austin Friars, EC2N 2HG
Soloman Lane is cornered in Austin Friars.

Austin Friars is named after an Augustinian priory located on the site until the sixteenth century and the dissolution of the monasteries.

Spooks: The Greater Good (2015)

Dir. Bhara Nalluri

Thames House, 12 Millbank, SW1P 4QE
The exterior shots of the MI5 headquarters were filmed at the real headquarters on Millbank.

Lambeth Bridge, Lambeth Road, SE1 7LB
Harry Pearce (Peter Firth) leaves MI5 and walks across Lambeth Bridge. He stands on the wall and contemplates suicide.

Athenaeum Club, 107 Pall Mall, St James's, SW1Y 5ER
When ex-agent Will Holloway (Kit Harington) returns from Moscow to help find Pearce, he reports directly to the Whitehall office which was filmed at the Athenaeum Club.

The Athenaeum Club was founded in 1824 and is a private members' club. The clubhouse has a frieze, designed by Decimus Burton and based on the Parthenon. Members have included artists Sir Lawrence Alma-Tadema and Sir Edward Burne-Jones, Benjamin Disraeli, and writer of Sherlock Holmes Sir Arthur Conan Doyle.

Nobel House, Millbank, SW1P 3HX
Geraldine (Jennifer Ehle) walks through Victoria Tower Gardens South speaking on the phone to Holloway. You can see Nobel House in the background. She discusses that she knows of a terrorist plot, and that Pearce and Qasim (Elyes Gabel) could be working together.

James Smith & Sons, Hazelwood House, 53 New Oxford Street, WC1A 1BL
The MI5 contact point was at this rather swanky umbrella shop. Holloway receives a note from Pearce with a clue of a man carrying an umbrella.

James Smith & Sons have been at this same location, making bespoke umbrellas and walking sticks since 1830.

Babington House, Redcross Way, SE1 1EZ
Holloway climbs onto the roof of Babington House in order to get into June's (Tuppence Middleton) flat via her balcony.

St Pancras Renaissance Hotel, Euston Road, NW1 2AR
Holloway picks Pearce up outside St Pancras Station and tells him he has identified one of the MI5 Leaks.

This iconic hotel was designed by George Gilbert Scott and was opened in 1873 as the Midland Grand Hotel.

The Grand hotel closed in 1935 and the building was taken over by the rail company for offices. It was once more closed in the 1980s after failing health and safety regulations. In 2011 it was re-opened as the St Pancras Renaissance Hotel.

James Smith & Sons, Hazelwood House, 53 New Oxford Street, WC1A 1BL

Noël Coward Theatre, 85-88 St Martin's Lane, WC2N 4AP
www.noelcowardtheatre.co.uk

The suicide bomb exploded at the Albery Theatre at a NATO gala killing Francis Warrender (David Harewood).

The exterior shots were taken at the Noël Coward Theatre on St Martin's Lane whereas the interior shots were filmed at the Gaiety Theatre on the Isle of Man.

The theatre was first opened in 1902 and Noël Coward made his debut at the theatre in his own play *I'll Leave It to You*. It has been an active theatre since it opened.

National Theatre, Upper Ground, SE1 9PX

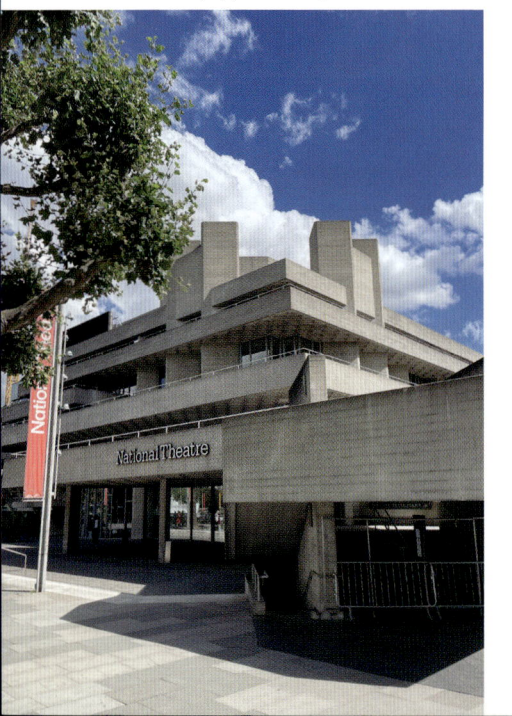

Fenchurch Street, EC3M 5JE
After being drugged by Oliver Mace (Tim McInnerny) Holloway wakes up in a car on Fenchurch Street turning into Lloyds Avenue.

3 Crutched Friars, EC3N 2HT
The car crashes outside Lutidine House meaning Holloway can escape down Rangoon Street.

National Theatre, Upper Ground, SE1 9PX
Qasim (Elyes Gabel) places a sniper on the third-floor concrete terrace of the National Theatre and shoots Hannah Santo (Eleanor Matsuura).

Tinker Tailor Soldier Spy (2011)

Dir. Tomas Alfredson

Blythe House, 23 Blythe Road, West Kensington, W14 0QX
'The Circus', an abbreviation of Cambridge Circus, is the headquarters of the British Intelligence Service which was filmed in Blythe House. The office which was located in the courtyard had been added by CGI for the film.

Blythe House was built for the Post Office Savings Bank in 1903. It currently is a storage unit for the Victoria and Albert and the Science museums.

Hampstead No.1 Pond, Hampstead Heath, NW5 1QR
George Smiley (Gary Oldman) swims in the Mixed Bathing Pond (NW5 1QR) and walks past Pond number 1.

18 Lloyd Square, Islington, WC1X 9AJ
George Smiley (Gary Oldman) lives at this address, although in the film it was meant to be 18 Asherton Street, N1.

(2) Wilkin Street, NW5 3NL
Mendell (Roger Lloyd-Pack), Smiley and Guillam (Benedict Cumberbatch) set up headquarters in a hotel near Liverpool Street. They are looking for the mole.

This was filmed in Wilkin Street but St Paul's Cathedral was added digitally in post-production.

Queen Alexandra's House, Bremner Road, South Kensington, SW7 2QT
The external shots for the control's (John Hurt) flat was filmed here.

This building has been student accommodation for the Royal College of Music, Art and Science since 1884.

Inglis Barracks, Mill Hill, NW7 1FE
The missing Jim Prideaux (Mark Strong) starts teaching at a school. His class is interrupted by a bird flying down the chimney, which he has no qualms with putting out of its misery in front of the kids. The school was filmed at the officers' mess at the Inglis Barracks.

Much of the barracks here have been refurbished into flats, but this building does remain intact.

18 Lloyd Square, Islington, WC1X 9AJ

6 TERRORISM

Criminal (2016)

Dir. Ariel Vromen

9 Royal Exchange, EC3V 3LL

Bill Pope (Ryan Reynolds) walks down Royal Exchange and enters the Gucci shop which at the time was situated at number 9.

24 Grosvenor Square, W1A 1AE

The former US Embassy on Grosvenor Square was used for the external shots of the American Embassy.

The embassy moved from Grosvenor Square in January 2018 after being on the site since 1960.

Bank Underground Station, Bank/Monument Complex, Princes Street, EC3V 3LA

Pope runs down the right-hand entrance to Bank Station in front of the Royal Exchange to try and shake off the people following him. He then leaves by another exit and jumps in a black cab and drives up Lombard Street.

Chimney Memorial, 23 Wesley Avenue, E16 1UR

Pope's taxi was diverted to the Spillers Factory where the chimney can be seen alongside it. The taxi driver was shot in the head, and Pope kidnapped.

The factory is still there and can be seen when standing by the chimney on Wesley Avenue although it is no longer possible to access the site.

Bank Tube, Cornhill, EC3V 3LR

Borough Market, Southwark Street, SE1 1TL

Chicken Run, 42 Toynbee Street, E1 7NE

Jerico Stewart (Kevin Costner), after escaping the police steals a kebab from Chicken Run on Toynbee Street. He then steals the van from the alley just down the side of the chicken shop.

Borough Market, SE1 9AL

Jerico is in a patisserie on Bedale Street where he punches a man in the face before heading into the market and regaining more memories.

SOAS University of London Library, Russell Square, WC1H 0XG

After regaining memories in Borough Market, he heads to the SOAS Library, which they refer to as the London Public Library. He then logs into Bill Pope's CIA account.

95 Stephen Road, E15 3JJ

On the corner with Meath Road, Jerico runs his van into Dr Micah Franks (Tommy Lee Jones) and pins him against SY Barbers on the corner.

London City Airport, North Woolwich, Hartmann Road, E16 2PX

The Dutchman (Michael Pitt) was spotted at London City Airport and the CIA rushed there to try to apprehend him.

Connaught Bridge, Silvertown, E16 2BU

There is a shoot out on the moving bridge, between the CIA, and those working for the Spanish anarchist, Xavier Heimdahl (Jordi Molla). Jerico drives the car off the bridge and into the river.

St Botolph-without-Bishopsgate, Bishopsgate, EC2M 3TL

Heimdahl's headquarters is at this church. The exterior shots were filmed here.

The current church on the site was built in 1729 and is the fourth on the site. The infant son of Elizabethan playwright, Ben Johnson is buried here.

Profile (2018)

Dir. Timur Bekmambetov

11 Mentmore Terrace, E8 3PN

The house where journalist, Amy Whittaker (Valene Kane) lives and takes the calls to jihadist Bilel (Shazad Latif) is on the top floor of this building and is opposite London Fields Overground station. Bilel and ISIS had reverse engineered her location when they issued a fatwa against her.

Jamme Masjid, Brick Lane, E1 6QL

When Matt (Morgan Watkins) Facetimes Amy following the death of Bilel he is walking down Brick Lane and it is possible to see the structure of the Jamme Masjid in the background.

The Crying Game (1992)

Dir. Neil Jorden

3 Fournier Street, E1 6QE
Millie's Hairdressing Salon where Fergus (Stephen Rea) checks up on Dil (Jaye Davidson) was filmed at 3 Fournier Street.

At the time of filming it was an empty building and today it is a 5-bedroomed residential property which sold for £3.6m in 2018.

Lilian Knowles House, Sanctuary Students, 47-50 Crispin Street, E1 6HQ
The old Crispin Street Women's Refuge building was the location for Fergus' (Stephen Rea) digs.

The refuge was originally built in 1868 and closed in the 1970s and offered a safe home for 300 women and children, and 50 men. The building is now student accommodation.

Ten Bells Pub, 84 Commercial Street, E1 6LY
www.tenbells.com

This was the local pub of many of the killer's victims.

This pub is open daily for beer, wine and cocktails.

Shoreditch Balls, 333 Old Street, EC1V 9LE
www.shoreditchballs.com

Lilian Knowles House, Sanctuary Students, 47-50 Crispin Street, E1 6HQ

The interior shots of the 'Metro Bar', where Dil sings, was filmed here. At the time of filming it was the London Apprentice. Today it is Shoreditch Balls and combines food, drink and mini-golf.

8-9 Hoxton Square, N1 6NU
www.happinessforgets.com

Dil lived at number 8-9 Hoxton Square and we see Fergus watching him.
    The site is now a cocktail bar called Happiness Forgets and is open every evening.

124-126 Brick Lane, E1 6RU
Irish terrorist Jude (Miranda Richardson) spies on the couple at the Indian restaurant, filmed on Brick Lane.
    This was shot at the now closed Preem & Prithi Balti House which is now Enso, a Thai and Japanese fusion restaurant.

37 Chesham Street, SW1X 8NQ
Dil follows Fergus to the Lowndes Arms pub on Chesham Street. This pub is now private residential property with no signs of its former use.

100 Eaton Place, SW1X 8LW
The judge was attacked at a discreet brothel at 100 Eaton Place. There is no indication this is its use in real life!

Coronet Street, between Hoxton Square and Boot Street, EC1V 9LA
The exterior shot of the Metro Bar was filmed on this stretch of road.

V for Vendetta (2005)

Dir. James McTeigue

Cloth Fair, Smithfield, EC1A 7JQ
Evey (Natalie Portman) is walking down Cloth Fair after curfew when she is apprehended by three Fingermen. She is rescued by the masked figure of V (Hugo Weaving) who kills them all with a sword.
    Cloth Fair as the name would suggest was used in the medieval period by cloth merchants selling their wares during the Bartholomew Fair. Number 41/42 is the oldest house in the City of London, and was built between 1597 and 1614.

Giltspur Street, EC1A 7AA
V takes Evey to the roof to enjoy a 'musical event'. Tchaikovsky's 1812 Overture is played over the loudspeakers in the street. This was filmed on Giltspur Street

Rawstorne Street, Finsbury, EC1V 7AJ
During the musical event, the people on Rawstorne Street left their homes and looked out the windows to see what was happening.

Old Bailey, EC4M 7EH
At the crescendo of the musical display the Old Bailey was blown up starting with the gilt-bronze statue of Justice.
    This statue was created by sculptor F.E. Pomeroy in 1905-1906. It portrays

Lady Justice, who would normally be blindfolded to show a lack of prejudice.

Piccadilly Circus, W1V 9LB
On the corner of Shaftesbury Avenue the LED screens broadcast propaganda films created by Adam Sutler (John Hurt). This is also where V makes the first 'V TV' broadcast from the BTN offices.

Farringdon Tube Station, Cowcross Street, EC1M 6BY
Child Evey is shown with her parents outside Farringdon Tube distributing anti-viral weapons leaflets. This scene was filmed at the Cowcross Street Entrance.

6 Alwyne Road, N1 2HH
Evey tricks the bishop (John Standing) and returns to Gordon Dietrich's (Stephen Fry) home. He shows her his secret collection of anti-government propaganda and banned books. He tells her, 'If the government searched my house she [*Evey*] would be the least of my worries'.

He is also later arrested from this address.

Farringdon Tube Station, Cowcross Street, EC1M 6BY

Thornhill Crescent, N1 1BL

The coroner, Dr Delia Surridge (Sinéad Cusack), is on V's hit list as she once worked at the Larkhill detention facility. She lives on Thornhill Crescent although the number isn't clear.

The police drive with sirens wailing into the street from the Crescent Street junction.

Aldwych Station, Surrey Street, WC2R 2ND
www.ltmuseum.co.uk/hidden-london

In Valerie's flashback as the journalists are reporting on the war the boarded-up Strand Station is in the background. This is the original entrance to Aldwych Station.

Also at Aldwych Station, on the abandoned platform, V reveals to Evey that the train full of explosives will travel via the tunnels to detonate under the Houses of Parliament.

Aldwych Station was officially closed in 1994, as it was not cost effective to renovate it. However, it has been used as a filming location since then and is occasionally opened to the public for specialist tours run by the London Transport Museum.

Bridgeman Road, N1 1BN

Guy Fawkes's masks are delivered to everyone in London. The delivery driver heads to Thornhill Crescent along Bridgeman Road.

Chalk Farm footbridge, Regent's Park Road, NW1 8JA

Police inspector Eric Finch (Stephen Rea) does a voiceover of how it all stemmed back to Larkhill. One of the accompanying scenes shows a young girl in a Guy Fawkes' mask, writing on a wall before she is shot dead by a Fingerman. This took place on the Chalk Farm Footbridge. The Fingerman is then attacked and beaten to the floor.

Trafalgar Square, WC2N 5DN

Hundreds of masked protesters appear from behind the central fountain in Trafalgar Square, and march together across Westminster Bridge and down Whitehall. The most sinister flash mob going.

Whitehall, SW1 2AY

The military guard Whitehall from the thousands of protesters, but eventually are overcome by sheer numbers.

This scene was filmed over three nights.

Houses of Parliament, Bridge Street, SW1A 2PW

The train packed with explosives explodes under the Houses of Parliament in time to the music (Tchaikovsky's 1812 Overture) as the masses all remove their masks at once.

7

MISCELLANEOUS CRIMES

Some films don't fit easily into the other sub-genres defined so far in this book, or they cross genres. For example, a number of films on drugs could cross over into gangland, murder or robbery depending on the sub-plot of the film. There are other films, which while crime is the essence of the film like *Carry on Constable*, they don't easily sit with other films already discussed or the St Trinian franchise where the crime isn't necessarily the main focus of the film. A few of these misfit films are placed in this section.

Carry On Constable (1960)

Dir. Gerald Thomas

Hanwell Library, Cherington Road, Hanwell, W7 3HL

The police station as the main set of *Carry on Constable* was filmed at Hanwell Library. This was one of the 660 libraries built by Andrew Carnegie, a Scottish-American businessman and philanthropist. These were all built between 1883 and 1929.

St Mary's Church, Church Road, Hanwell, W7 3BZ

PC Gorse (Charles Hawtry) helps a distraught mother (Irene Handl) look for her lost cat Willie. He starts the search outside 12 Lothair Road (W5 4TA), ending up at St Mary's Church, where in true *Carry On* style he gets trapped in the steeple. I mean, how do such things happen?

Clockwork Orange (1971)

Dir. Stanley Kubrick

Brunel University, Uxbridge, UB8 3PH

Brunel University was used for the location of the entrance of Alex's (Malcom McDowell) block of flats. Tower D, is one of four engineering and design Department buildings.

The 'Ludovico Medical Facility', where Alex goes through aversion therapy was filmed at the Lecture Centre.

The Brunel University buildings were new at the time of filming as they were completed between 1966 and 1971. They are Grade II listed buildings as representative of the brutalist style.

Southern Underpass, Trinity Road, Wandsworth, SW18 1GS

The Droogs attack an Irish homeless man in a subway at Wandsworth roundabout where it connects Trinity Road and Swandon Way.

Southmere Lake, Thamesmead, SE2 9AN

A lot of Clockwork Orange was filmed in Thamesmead which was 'new' at the time. Since filming the area has gone through a renovation.

However, some places still remain including the 'Flat Block Marina' which was filmed at the artificial Southmere Lake. This was where Alex pushes Dim (Warren Clarke) under the water.

McDonald's, Kings Road, SW3 4ND

Alex heads to a record shop on the King's Road and chats up two girls.

In 1971, it was the Chelsea Drugstore. Now it is McDonald's and the large windows have been filled with advertising posters.

Chelsea Embankment, Oakley Street, Chelsea, SW3 5NN

Following Alex's cure, he bumps into one of his previous victims at Chelsea Embankment. They pay him back under Albert Bridge.

Wandsworth Prison, Heathfield Road, SW18 3HR

Alex was incarcerated at Parkmoor Prison for murder for 14 years.

The exterior shots were filmed at Wandsworth prison.

Death Defying Acts (2007)

Dir. Gillian Armstrong

Wilton's Music Hall, 1 Graces Alley, E1 8JB

www.wiltons.org.uk

This was where, Harry Houdini (Guy Pearce) performed his act.

Wilton's Music Hall was built in 1859 by architect Jacob Maggs and has had an interesting history. It caught fire in 1878 and had to be rebuilt. It is one of the few saloon-style music halls still in its original form and was reopened as a performance venue in 1997.

Green Street (2005)

Dir. Lexi Alexander

East Finchley Underground Station, High Road, N2 0NW

The opening scene on the platform at 'Bank Station' was filmed at East Finchley instead. Bank is all underground, whereas these platforms were above ground. If you look in the background, you will see the Underground signs have actually been blanked out. This platform was later used when Matt Bruckner (Elijah Wood) was leaving the tube.

MISCELLANEOUS CRIMES | 121

Bank Underground Station, Royal Exchange, EC3V 3LR
The fight continues outside the real Bank Underground Station, and you can see the Royal Exchange in the background.

Paddington Station, Praed Street, W2 1HU
As Matt travels to London, he gets off the train at Paddington where he goes down the escalator towards the Bakerloo Line. Later in the film the Green Street Elite (GSE) meet here before heading to platform 5 to take a train to see West Ham play away in Manchester.

FYI trains from Paddington don't go to Manchester.

101 Cadogan Square, SW1X 0DY
After leaving the station, Matt and his sister, Shannon (Claire Forlani) walk along Cadogan Square to her flat at number 101. If you look very carefully you will see the Blue Plaque at number 75 marking where the novelist Arnold Bennett lived.

The Griffin, Brook Road South, Brentford, TW8 0NP
www.griffinbrentford.co.uk

Pete (Charlie Hunnam) takes Matt to The Griffin before his first football match, approaching it from Braemar Road. In the pub, Matt is introduced to Pete's football friends and learns it is the headquarters of the Green Street Elite (GSE).

The Griffin is open daily for food and drink.

Corbett's Lane, SE16 2BE
Following the football match there is a fight in and around Silwood Street and Corbett's Lane. On Corbett's Lane, the arch with 'No Parking' written on it, was where they all jumped in the van before a brick was thrown through the windscreen.

The area has been redeveloped since the film was made in 2005, but the arches are still there.

Fenchurch Street Station, Fenchurch Place, EC3M 4AJ
This is used to represent Manchester's train station where the gang were waiting for the GSE to arrive and is where they have a massive fight.

Rotherhithe Tunnel, SE16 5QJ
Bovver (Leo Gregory) heads through the Rotherhithe Tunnel on his motor bike on the way to Millwall.

City View Hotel, 11 Church Street, E15 3HU
Bovver waits outside the King's Head pub, on the corner of Church Street and Church Street North.

This pub has now been redeveloped into the 11 City View Hotel.

8 Church Street, E15 3HX
Bovver waits outside a café at number 8 Church Street before having an altercation with the Millwall gang. Number 8 is currently Selmo's café although it is permanently closed. The exterior appears to have gone through a refurb since the film was made.

New Moon Pub, Leadenhall Market, Gracechurch Street, EC3V 1LT
www.newmoonleadenhall.com

Matt speaks with his dad (Henry Goodman) when he finds out he was thrown out of Harvard. They were sitting outside the New Moon Pub before walking towards the Gracechurch Street entrance.

They are open Monday to Saturday for food and drinks. They are closed on Sunday.

40 Lime Street, EC3M 7AW
Matt is seen by the GSE entering the Times building with his father. They assume he is an undercover journalist. The GSE member on his bike is at the bottom of the steps of the building opposite.

Layer Cake (2004)

Dir. Matthew Vaughn

44 Formosa Street, W9 2JS
The narrator (Daniel Craig) starts the film with a voice over explaining his cocaine business. The visuals show him walking down Formosa Street, past the St Saviour's C of E primary School.

His estate agents can be found at number 44 Formosa Street and is currently an estate agent called Braithwait.

7 Queen's Gate Mews, Kensington, SW7 5QJ
The narrator lives at this address and is picked up here for an appointment with Jimmy Price (Kenneth Cranham).

Regency Cafe, 17-19 Regency Street, SW1P 4BY
The narrator and Morty (George Harris) meet in this café. As the narrator is at the counter getting tea, Freddy (Ivan Kaye) joins them, eating a full English before Morty rearranges his face.

St Martin's Lane Hotel, 45 St Martin's Lane, WC2N 4HX
The narrator invites Tammy (Sienna Miller) to St Martin's Hotel. However, as she prepares for an evening of fun, his evening takes an unusual turn as he is abducted in a laundry trolley.

1 West India Quay, Isle of Dogs, E14 4ED
When the narrator's blindfold is removed, he is startled to find himself upside-down and hanging from the roof of a half-built high-rise by Eddie Temple's (Michael Gambon) henchmen.

This building is the Marriott Executive Apartments.

107 Pall Mall, St James's, SW1Y 5ER
The narrator and Temple (Michael Gambon) meet in the library of the Athenaeum Club.

The Athenaeum Club was founded in 1824 and is a private members' club.

St Martin's Lane Hotel, 45 St Martin's Lane, WC2N 4HX

The clubhouse has a frieze, designed by Decimus Burton and based on the Parthenon. Members have included artists Sir Lawrence Alma-Tadema and Sir Edward Burne-Jones, Benjamin Disraeli, and writer of Sherlock Holmes, Sir Arthur Conan Doyle.

Paddington Station, Praed Street, W2 1HB
The narrator meets the hitman Mr Lucky (Paul Orchard) at Paddington Station in an attempt to avoid the Serbian, Dragan (Dragan Mićanović).

Paddington Station has been redeveloped since the film was made but the main structure is still there.

Royal Observatory, Blackheath Avenue, SE10 8XJ
The narrator agrees to meet Dragan at the statue of General Wolfe at the Royal Observatory in Greenwich Park. He arrives with an assassin, but it doesn't go according to plan.

The statue of General Wolfe was built in 1930 to commemorate his victory over the French in Quebec in the 18th century. Wolfe lived in Greenwich and is buried locally.

Sherlock Holmes (2009)

Dir. Guy Ritchie

Middle Temple Lane, EC4Y 9AA
Inspector Lestrade (Eddie Marsan) and Dr Watson (Jude Law) drive in a carriage through Temple, starting their journey on Middle Temple Lane.

Crossness Pumping Station, Abbey Wood, SE2 9AQ
www.crossness.org.uk

The spiral staircase leading into the crypt was filmed at the Crossness Pumping Station.

The pumping station was built by Sir Joseph Bazalgette in 1865. It is a museum which is open to the public.

Priory Church of St Bartholomew the Great, Cloth Fair, Barbican, EC1A 7JQ

Holmes (Robert Downey Jr) and Watson interrupt Lord Blackwood (Mark Strong) who is in the middle of preparing a human sacrifice in the Priory Church.

The Reform Club, Pall Mall, SW1Y 5EW

Holmes meets Watson and his soon to be fiancée, Mary (Kelly Reilly) at the Royale. Holmes analyses her until she retaliated by throwing a glass of wine in his face. This scene was filmed at the Reform Club.

The Reform Club was founded in 1836 for those who supported the Great Reform Act (1832). It was a private members' club, and in 1838 they employed a celebrity chef, Alexis Soyer. Their members include Winston Churchill, Arthur Conan Doyle and Camilla, when she was duchess of Cornwall. The Reform Club was the first private members' club to open its doors to women, in 1981.

Old Royal Naval College, King William Walk, SE10 9NN

General shots of olde worlde London were filmed at the Old Royal Naval College in Greenwich, as well as the exteriors of The Grand Hotel, Piccadilly. However, there was a lot of post-production CGI added to the scenes so it could be hard to match them with the reality of what is there.

Brompton Cemetery, Old Brompton Road, SW5 9JE

Lord Blackwood was buried in the Blackwood family vault following his death although he had been spotted strolling the cemetery. Holmes and Watson meet the police in front of the chapel in order to examine in detail the destroyed mausoleum in front of the colonnade. CGI additions had also been made to the colonnade.

College of Arms, 130 Queen Victoria Street, EC4V 4BT

Sir Thomas (James Fox) dies in the bathtub in his house. The exterior shots were filmed at the College of Arms.

The College of Arms is the official heraldic authority for the UK and the Commonwealth. It was founded in 1484 and has the responsibility for issuing coats of arms, registers of arms, pedigrees, genealogies, and changes of name and flags.

Freemasons' Hall, 60 Great Queen Street, WC2B 5AZ

www.ugle.org.uk/freemasons-hall/visit-freemasons-hall

Lord Blackwood oversees a Masonic meeting held in the Third Vestibule of the Freemasons' Hall.

Freemasons' Hall has stood on Great Queen Street since 1775 and has a small museum which is open to the public.

College of Arms, 130 Queen Victoria Street, EC4V 4BT (courtesy of philafrenzy, Wikimedia Commons)

Schiller International University, 51-55 Waterloo Road, SE1 8TX

Dr Watson is being cared for at the Royal Veterans' Hospital, following the explosion. The exterior shots were a combination of the Schiller University and post-production CGI.

Sherlock Holmes: A Game of Shadows (2011)

Dir. Guy Ritchie

Old Royal Naval College, Greenwich, SE10 9NN

General shots of Olde Worlde London were filmed at the Old Naval College in Greenwich and is where Holmes (Robert Downey Jr) follows Irene Adler (Rachel McAdams).

Irene avoids a booby-trapped package at the Cromwell and Griff Auction House, the exterior shots of which were also filmed at the Naval College.

Holmes fights with Irene's bodyguards in the covered walkway alongside the Queen's House, also in Greenwich.

Australia House, Strand, WC2B 4LA

Interior shots of the Cromwell and Griff Auction House were filmed here at Australia House.

Australia House was built in 1913 by Alexander Marshall Mackenzie and his son, Alexander George Robert Mackenzie. It was officially opened

Old Royal Naval College, Greenwich, King William Walk, SE10 9NN

by George V in 1918 as the diplomatic mission of Australia in the UK. It was built over a 900-year-old well which draws water from the River Fleet and is still considered safe to drink.

Wilton's Music Hall, 1 Grace's Alley, E1 8JB
www.wiltons.org.uk

Dr Watson (Jude Law) holds his stag night in the Theatre of Varieties, which was filmed at Wilton's Music Hall.

Wilton's Music Hall was built in 1859 by architect Jacob Maggs and has had an interesting history. It caught fire in 1878 and had to be rebuilt. It is one of the few saloon-style music halls still in its original form and was reopened as a performance venue in 1997.

Undercroft, Old Square, Lincoln's Inn, WC2A 3TL
The cellar of the Parisian Hotel where Holmes discovers there was a secret printing press was filmed in the Undercroft beneath the chapel.

The Undercroft is actually open to the elements and there was some nifty set-dressing to make it look like it was

MISCELLANEOUS CRIMES | 127

St Trinian's – The Great St Trinian's Train Robbery (1966)

Dirs. Sidney Gilliat and Frank Launder

15 Palace Court, W2 4LP
The Minister of Schools, Sir Horacce (Raymond Huntly) walks down Palace Court on his way to visit the headmistress of St Trinian's School. He continues walking until he meets the junction with Moscow Road. Today, the flats he was filmed walking past (opposite number 15) have been gated off and parking at the junction has been extended to the middle of the road.

15 Palace Court, W2 4LP

subterranean. The Lincoln's Inn Chapel was designed by Inigo Jones in 1623.

St Trinian's – Blue Murder at St Trinian's (1957)

Dir. Frank Launder

1 Great George Street, SW1P 3AA
Some girls from St Trinian's break into the Ministry of Education to swap out the papers to ensure they win a UNESCO prize to travel to Europe. This government building is number 1 Great George Street.

The Criminal (1999)

Dir. Julian Simpson

Queen Mary and Westfield's College, 327 Mile End Road, Bethnal Green, E1 4NS
Jasper (Steven Mackintosh) lived in Fabian Court. This was filmed at the side entrance of Queen Mary and Westfield's College through the gates to the right.

Savoy Steps (behind The Coal Hole Pub) Aldwych, WC2R 0EX
This was the site of the final revelations and the tying up of loose ends.
 Bob Dylan filmed the video for *Subterranean Homesick Blues* (1965) near these steps with the iconic cards and the lyrics.

Institute of Director's Club, 116 Pall Mall, St James's, SW1Y 5ED
The Brasserie here was transformed into a lowly café where DI Walker (Bernard Hill) talks to rent boy, Jonny (Daniel Brocklebank).

Waterlow Park, Highgate Hill, N6 5HG
This is where Peter Hume (Eddie Izzard) meets with the man on the run Jasper Rawlins (Steven Mackintosh).

Café Lazeeze, 88 St John Street, Farringdon, EC1M 4EH
This was 'Slammers' where Jasper Rawlins looks for the barman Guy (Matthew Blackmore). He finds him dead in the gents.

Green Dragon Court, Borough, SE1 9AW
This is where Sarah Maitland's (Natasha Little) past is revealed in a flashback.

Bethnal Green Town Hall, Cambridge Heath Road, E2 9NF
The wood panelled office from *Lock Stock and Two Smoking Barrels*' 'Hatchet' Harry is also the police station in *The Criminal*.
 The Town Hall has since been developed into a hotel.

Underwood Street (near Nile Street), N1 7LG
Jasper Rawlins was bundled into the peepshow on this street.

The Football Factory (2004)

Dir. Nick Love

Seven Sisters Tube Station, Seven Sisters Road, Tottenham, N15 5LA
Fans are shown leaving the tube station onto Seven Sisters Road.

Birstall Road, N15 5EN
Billy Bright (Frank Harper) and his gang turn off Seven Sisters Road into Birstall Road.

Harwood Arms, Walham Grove, SW6 1QJ
www.harwoodarms.com

Bill (Dudley Sutton) and Albert (John Junkin) catch the taxi outside the pub to take them to the dancing venue.

This upmarket pub is open daily for lunch and dinner and may require a reservation.

St Alban's Terrace, W6 8HJ
This is where Bill and Albert leave the racist taxi driver to go dancing.

Piccadilly Circus, SW1Y 4QF
Tommy (Danny Dyer) and Rod (Neil Maskell) run though Piccadilly Circus from the pub when the cup draw is announced, being chased by the guy Rod had hit with a cricket bat.

Queen's Elm, 241 Fulham Road, SW3 6HY
Tommy buys flowers for Albert's funeral in front of this pub. The pub closed in the 1990s and has been divided into a number of retail units.

Millwall Football Ground, Senegal Road, SE16 3LP
At the start of the Millwall-Chelsea game there are shots outside the football ground of all the fans arriving.

Piccadilly Circus, W1V 9LB

Millwall Football Ground, Senegal Road, SE16 3LP

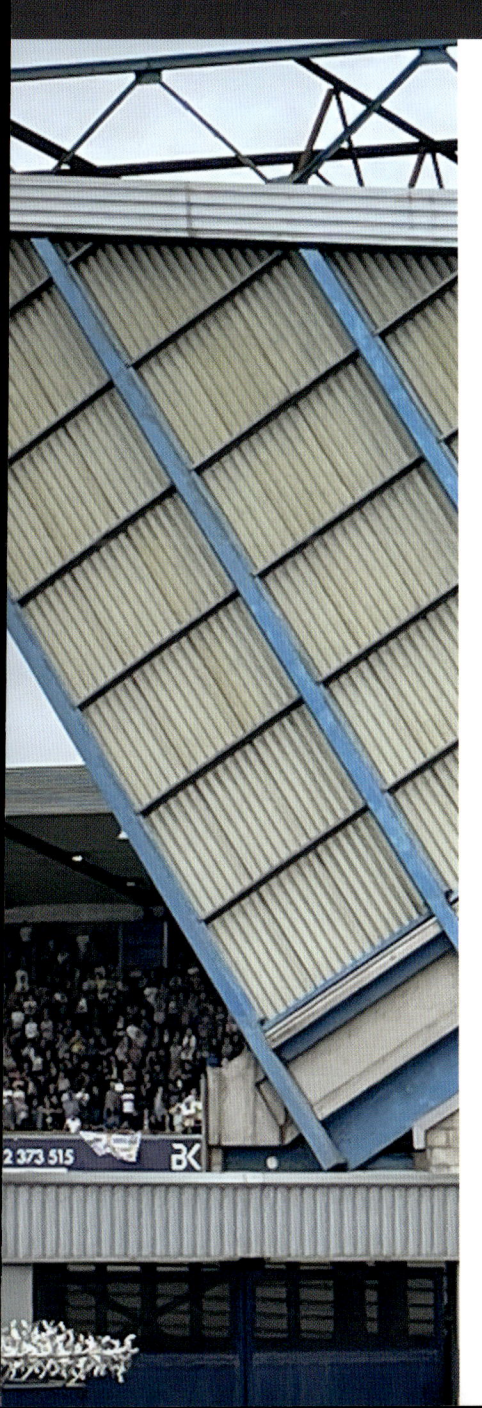

MISCELLANEOUS CRIMES | 131

Surrey Quays Tube, Rotherhithe Old Road Entrance, SE16 2PP
Tommy and the gang were seen leaving Surrey Quays tube to start the fight with the Millwall fans on match day.

122 Oldfield Grove Road, SE16 2NE
As the gang walk for what seems like miles over a bridge which has since been reconfigured, they walk past a yellow house which is now pink which is at 122 Oldfield Grove Road.

Above: Surrey Quays Tube, Rotherhithe Old Road Entrance, SE16 2PP

Below: 122 Oldfield Grove Road, SE16 2NE

Footbridge, Oldfield Grove Road, SE16 2NE

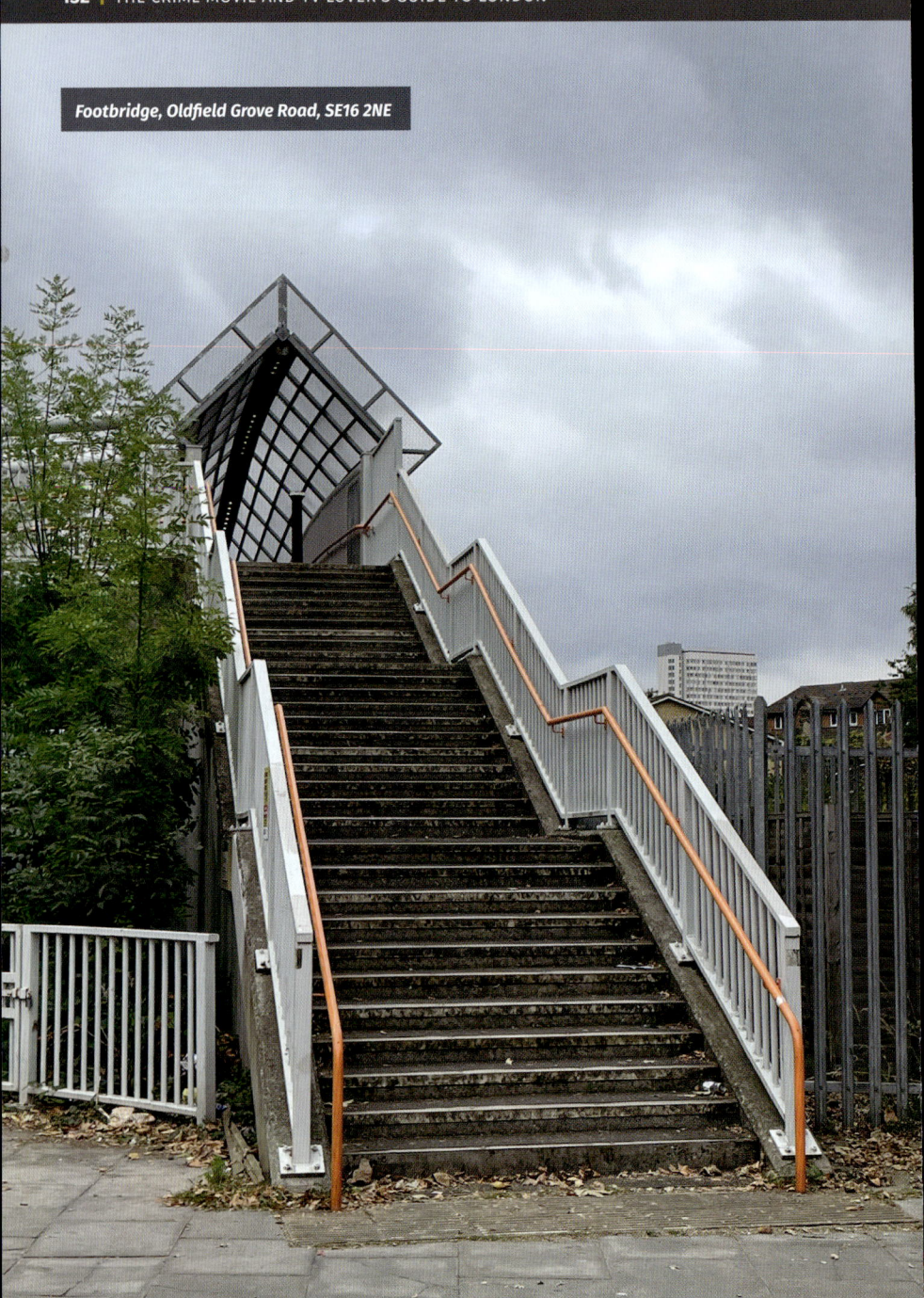

This pink house used to be the Baron Arms Pub and was closed in the 1980s and turned into flats. The bridge cost more than £3m to renovate.

55 Silwood Street, SE16 2AW
This is the closest address to the railway arch where the Millwall and Chelsea gang finally clash and where the police catch up and break the fight up but not before Tommy gets injured.

55 Silwood Street, SE16 2AW

Trainspotting (1996)

Dir. Danny Boyle

Talgarth Road, W14 9ES
Renton (Ewan McGregor) waits on the other side of the road to show his clients around the property which is on the junction of North End Road.
   Begbie (Robert Carlyle) and Sick Boy (Jonny Lee Miller) came to squat at Renton's flat. The exteriors were filmed here, just above Serenity Nails Salon.

Smallbrook Mews, Bayswater, W2 3BN
Sick Boy organised the buying and selling of heroin from Smallbrook Mews.

Royal Eagle Hotel, 26-30 Craven Road, W2 3QP
The gang meet the dealer (Keith Allen) with the heroin at the Royal Eagle Hotel on Craven Road.
   The interior shots were filmed at a hotel in Glasgow, but as Renton legs it out of the hotel with the money, it is the Royal Eagle Hotel.
   The building was empty when the filming was done but is now a much higher calibre hotel.

Gloucester Mews, W2 3HE
Renton walks into Gloucester Mews with the stolen money.

8
TV DRAMAS

TV dramas have enabled crime and the cosy crime sub-genre to enter our homes on a weekly basis and was often based on literature such as Agatha Christie with Poirot or Miss Marple, and Arthur Conan Doyle with Sherlock Holmes. Many of the detective-based dramas follow the same format as laid out by Christie with a big reveal at the end where the detective gathers everyone into a room to cleverly demonstrate how they did it. The police-led dramas such as *Silent Witness* only became popular in the 1990s when the public were becoming concerned with increasing violence and crime and was a means of showing the other side. Crime dramas don't seem to be losing their popularity and more are being released every year.

The Capture (TV Series, 2019-2022)

Creator: Ben Chanan

Central St Giles, WC2H 8AB
DS Patrick Flynn (Cavan Clerkin) arrives at the Truro Analytics offices which were located at Central St Giles.

St Magnus House Passageway, 3 Lower Thames Street, EC3R 6HD
DCI Rachel Carey (Holliday Grainger) is filmed walking towards the government building over this raised walkway.

Abingdon Street Car Park, Great College Street, SW1P 3RX
Isaac Turner (Paapa Essiedu) is driven away from the parliament building exiting via this car park.

140 London Wall, Barbican, EC2Y 5DN
Commander Hart (Ben Miles) sees DCI Carey whilst out jogging.

Sumner Street, SE1 9JA
Isaac Turner confronts Xanda's boss, Yan Wanglei (Rob Yang) here.

Excel London, Royal Victoria Dock, 1 Western Gateway, E16 1XL
Isaac Turner arrives for the presentation by Xanda.

29 Sclater Street, E1 6HT
DS Latif (Ginny Holder) meets DS Flynn outside the crime scene on Scalter Street. Edison Yao (Joshua Jo) is also seen entering the apartment block here.

BBC Broadcasting House, Langham Street, W1B 3DF
DCI Carey heads to the BBC before Newsnight was due to air. She enters the BBC with DSU Gemma Garland.

62 Buckingham Gate, SW1E 6AJ
Isaac Turner is at the Home Office which is filmed at this address. We see him arrive and then speed away shortly afterwards.

The Shard, 32 London Bridge Street, SE1 9SG
DI Rachel Carey and Commander Danny Hart meet in the Aqua Shard restaurant when he is eating with his family. She confronts him.

Printworks, Surrey Quays Road, SE16 7PJ
www.printworkslondon.co.uk

Internal shots were filmed here when DCI Carey was fleeing from two assailants through the corridors of the Printworks.

The Printworks is currently an event space which can be hired out.

Crime Traveller (TV Series, 1997)

Creator: Anthony Horowitz

St Mary's Mansions, St Mary's Terrace, Paddington, W2 1SU
Science Officer, Holly Turner's (Chloë Annett) flat was Sundown Court filmed on St Mary's Terrace and was next to Maddie's from *Jonathan Creek*. She was waiting for her bi-transmutor to be delivered, and it was in the porter's office when she got home. It appears in every episode as the location of the time machine.

The building is on the left hand of the corner leading to the gated community.

Café Laville, 453 Edgware Road, W2 1TH
This was the site of Giovanni's Café, where Holly Turner tells DI Jeff Slade (Michael French) about the time machine in the first episode and how she was able to retrieve the evidence from the lost luggage. He doesn't believe her, and she leaves upset.

In episode four, they are both eating here when Slade tells her that he knows she has time travelled back to be with him.

This restaurant overlooks the canal and serves Italian and Mediterranean food.

Woburn Walk, WC1H 0JL
In episode four Holly and Slade stood outside the jewellers (6A) and she tells him what will happen to him later is serious. They then enter the art gallery (12) to speak to Levenson about his relationship with the dead artist.

Alexandra and Ainsworth Estate, Rowley Way, Camden, NW8 0SN
In episode four this is where the jewel thief Crowley lives. Slade climbs up a

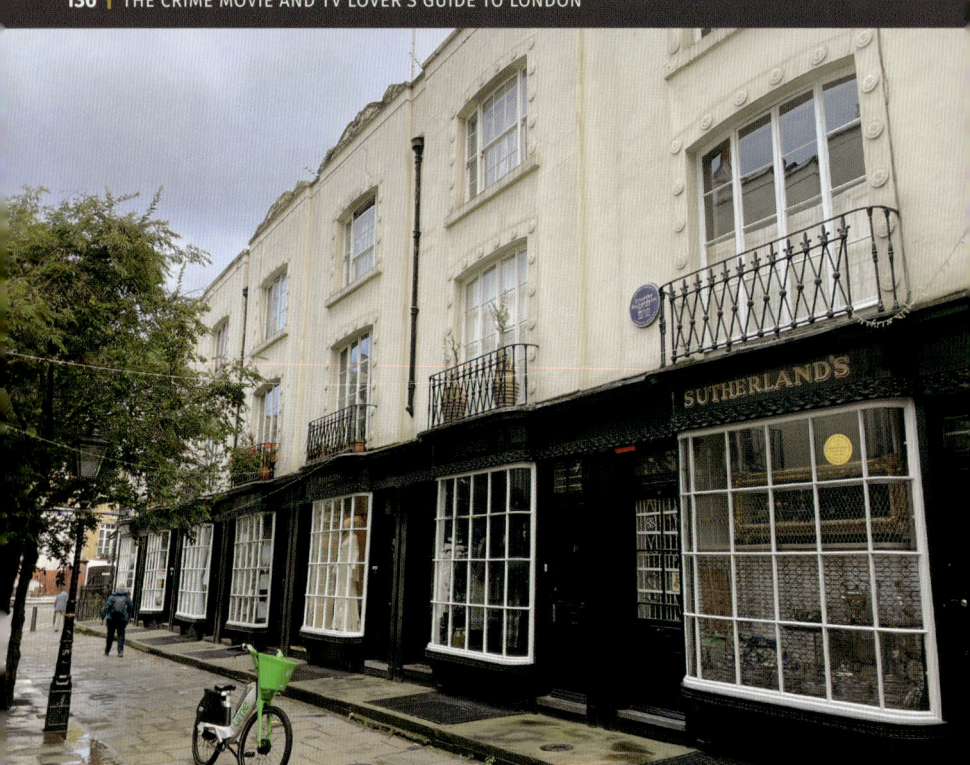

6A Woburn Walk, WC1H 0JL

fire escape ladder to the roof and drops down to a top floor balcony in order to enter Crowley's flat.

Landmark London, 222 Marylebone Road, NW1 6JQ

Slade scales the building on the Melcombe Place side of the Landmark, heading onto the glass ceiling of the atrium in episode five. He was chasing Leonard Gebler (Stephen Grief) who had stolen the diamonds. He is filmed in the glass atrium which is now the Winter Garden restaurant.

Sinclair House, 6 Hastings Street, WC1H 9PZ

Jeff, DS Morris (Paul Trussell), and Robson (Richard Dempsey) tail a suspect to Sherif's Snack Bar on the corner of Sandwich Street and Hastings Street.

The location is now the Sandwich Street Kitchen.

Renoir (now Curzon Bloomsbury), The Brunswick Centre, WC1N 1AW

Holly takes Jeff to the cinema to see *Les Enfants* in episode eight. Jeff wasn't as enthusiastic as Holly about the film.

Curzon Bloomsbury, The Brunswick Centre, WC1N 1AW

The Gold (TV Series, 2022)

Creator: Neil Forsyth

National Liberal Club, 1 Whitehall Place, SW1A 2HE
The interior shots of Kenny Noye's Mason club was filmed at the National Liberal Club.

Providence Square Lookout, 49 Bermondsey Wall W, SE1 2AX
This was the location of Edwyn Cooper's (Dominic Cooper) riverside apartment. The view of the building is better from the other side of the river.

Whittaker House, Richmond, TW9 1EH
This site was where the exterior shots for Guyerzeller Bank, Zurich where the meeting between DCI Brian Boyce (Hugh Bonneville) and the Swiss bank were held. They were hoping to find out the names of the owners of the bank accounts.

Heron Square, Richmond, TW9 1EH
This was another building which was meant to be in Switzerland and was the filming location for the office where they went to get the names.

The Ship & Whale, 2 Gulliver Street, SE16 7LT
www.shipandwhale.co.uk

Brian Boyce meets Edwyn Cooper here, and Gordon Parry (Sean Harris) tells them the gold is behind the bar. He asks Cooper to help him get it, before they do a runner out the back of the pub.

The pub was first built in 1767 but the present building is dated to the 1880s. They are open every evening for food and drinks and all day on Saturday and Sunday.

Jonathan Creek (TV Series, 1997–2016)

Creator: David Renwick

The Pagoda, Pagoda Gardens, Blackheath, SE3 0RE
This was the location of Hedley (Colin Baker) and Serena Shales's (Serena Gish) house where he was found brutally murdered in *The Wrestler's Tomb*.

Richmond Theatre, 1 Little Green, Richmond, TW9 1QJ
www.atgtickets.com/venues/richmond-theatre

This is where Adam Klaus (Anthony Head) performs his stage show in the first episode of *Jonathan Creek*.

Designed by architect Frank Matcham the Richmond Theatre was opened in 1899. It has been an active theatre since it opened.

St Mary's Mansions, St Mary's Terrace, Paddington, W2 1SU
This was the location of Maddie's (Caroline Quentin) flat and was where in *Jack in the Box* Jonathan (Alan

Davies) removes the wheel clamp from her car not realising she has the key.

Maddie's building is on the right hand of the corner leading to the gated community.

Lemonia, 89 Regent's Park Road, NW1 8UY
Maddie is having lunch with her agent at Lemonia in *The Reconstituted Corpse*, when she nips across the road to buy a wardrobe from Graham and Green which is still operating today.

85 Redchurch Street, E2 7DJ
This was the location of the derelict Mother Redcap in an episode of the same name, where a number of people had been murdered in a creative manner in the 1940s. Today it is a household goods shop called Labour and Wait.

156 Uxbridge Road, W12 8AA
In *Time Waits for Norman*, this was a Wimpy where everything falls into place for Jonathan.

Today it is Yogi Smurti Newsagents.

Sutton Court, Fauconberg Road, Chiswick, W4 3JU
This was the location of Maddie's flat, and where the two new men in her life both arrive for dinner in *The Eyes of Tiresias*.

Northcote Road, Battersea, SW11 1NP
The street scenes were filmed here where Adam Klaus (Stuart Milligan) is seen performing 'magic' for passers-by. The corner of Mallinson Road, and Oddono's Ice-Cream Shop is in the background.

Citypoint, 1 Ropemaker Street, Barbican, EC2V 9HT
In *The Chequered Box*, DI Adrian Fell (Colin McFarlane) is set up for a murder of a solicitor in this building.

Roundwood Park, Willesden Green, NW10 3SH
In *The Chequered Box*, Adam Klaus is crucified as part of a publicity stunt in Roundwood Park in Willesden Green.

University of Westminster, Harrow Campus, Watford Road, Northwick Park Roundabout, HA1 3TP
In *The Coonskin Cap*, Sgt Heather Davey (Anna Wilson-Jones) was murdered inside the gym on this university campus.

Covent Garden, Bedford Street, WC2E 9ED
In *The Tailor's Dummy*, Kenny Starkiss (Bill Bailey) does a dubious teleportation trick here in front of St Paul's Church.

Primrose Hill, NW3 3DS
Carla (Julia Sawalha) watches from the junction of Ainger Road and Primrose Hill Road, as Jonathan and Pam (Tamsin Greig) walk and play in the park in *Gorgon's Wood*.

187 Church Road, NW10 9EE
Whilst investigating in *Gorgon's Wood*, Jonathan Creek enters the Adult-O-Rama on the corner of Church Road and Preston Gardens and finds some boot-leg blow-up dolls of Carla Borrego.

This was the Dunya AFG Bakery but is now standing empty.

Jonathan Creek Special – The Judas Tree (2010)

Creator: David Renwick

Clayton Hotel, Chiswick High Road, W4 5RY
A bus stop was set up outside the Clayton Hotel for Jonathan and Emily Somerton (Natalie Walter) to meet.

Chiswick Town Hall, Heathfield Terrace, W4 4JN
Inside the Town Hall, Adam (Stuart Milligan) and Jonathan are practicing some tricks and Joey (Sheridan Smith) is roped in to help in *The Judas Tree*.

Killing Eve (TV Series, 2018–2022)

Creator: Phoebe Waller-Bridge

Season One

4 Warwick House Street, St James's, SW1Y 5BN
In season one, this was used for the external shots of the Task Force offices.

Bill (David Haig) and Eve (Sandra Oh) are seen walking towards the office talking about the potential killings that have taken place.

Guy's Hospital, SE1 9GU
Eve finds Bill after he had left the office to Guy's Campus, where he tries to get her to reveal the motive for the assassinations.

The Albert, 52 Victoria Street, SW1H 0NP
www.greeneking.co.uk/pubs/greater-london/albert

Bill and Eve talk to Frank about the CCTV footage.
The pub is open daily for food and drink.

Fabric, 77A Charterhouse Street, EC1M 6HJ
The Berlin club where Bill was killed on the dance floor was filmed at Fabric on Charterhouse Street.

Hampstead Parish Church, 14 Church Row, NW3 6UU
Bill's funeral was held in this church and following Frank's (Darren Boyd) terrible speech Eve leaves her old job in season one.

A church has been on the site since 1312 when John de Neuport is named as priest. In the eighteenth century part of the church was still timber so money was raised to rebuild in more durable stone. Further additions and beautifications were made in the later nineteenth century.

Guy's Hospital, SE1 9GU

Clapton Hart Pub, 231 Lower Clapton Road, E5 8EG
www.claptonhart.com

Bill's wake was held in this pub.
    They are open daily for food and drink.

Goldsmiths' Hall, Foster Lane, EC2V 6BN
Villanelle (Jody Comer) goes undercover and passes herself off as a caterer, with the aim of completing an assassination using perfume.

Hornsey Town Hall, The Broadway, N8 9JJ
This was used for the location of Eve and Carolyn's (Fiona Shaw) hotel, the Atlasov, in Moscow where they have the breakfast buffet.

Season Two

St George-in-the-East Crypt West, 14 Cannon Street Road, E1 0BH
Carolyn meets Eve in the cemetery of this church in season two.
    This church was built between 1714 and 1729 by Nicholas Hawksmoor. The original interior of the church was damaged when it was hit by a bomb in the Blitz and was replaced in the 1960s.

Charing Cross Underground, Strand, WC2N 5HF
Eve considers pushing a passenger who had walked into her nearly knocking her onto the track as she adjusts her bulletproof vest in season two. This

Tate Modern, Bankside, SE1 9TG

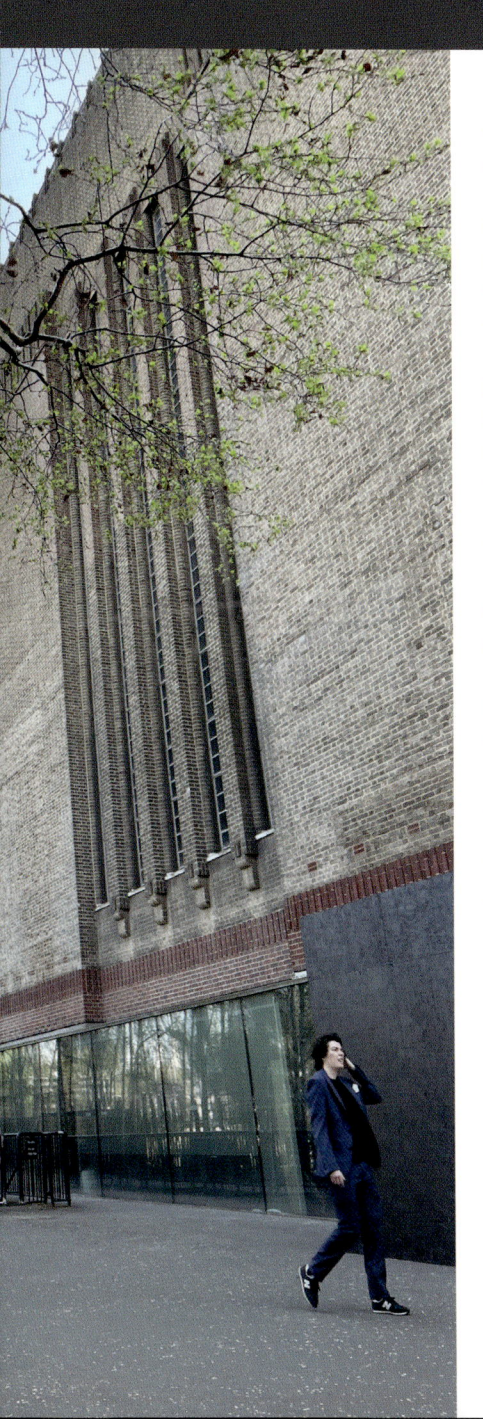

was filmed on the Jubilee Line platform, which was closed to the public in 1999.

Tate Modern, Bankside, SE1 9TG
Konstantin (Kim Bodnia) discovers Villanelle trying to out-stare a human statue outside the Tate.

Barbican Centre (Plaza) Silk Street, Barbican, EC2Y 8DS
Carolyn tells Eve on the Plaza that she still has her job.

147 Cromwell Road, SW5 0TH
The exterior shots for the Paddington hotel where Villanelle is staying were filmed here.

Barbican Launderette, 2 Fann Street, Barbican, EC2Y 8AF
While doing her laundry Villanelle falls asleep and her drugs are stolen.

Thames Path, Blackfriars Station, Southern Concourse, Hopton Street, SE1 9JH
Konstantin pays Villanelle for the last assassination she carried out and manages to avoid another run-in with a human statue.
    As you come out the station turn left and head under the bridge to the spot where it was filmed.

Russell Square, WC1B 4JA
Villanelle who is dressed as a schoolteacher follows Eve through Russell Square before she sees Raymond (Adrian Scarborough).

Barbican Crescent, Silk Street, EC2Y 8HD

Russell Square, WC1B 4JA

Four Seasons Hotel, 10 Trinity Square, EC1A 1BB
Villanelle believes she has killed Eve in the Royal Garden Suite of Four Seasons Hotel, Trinity Square.

The London Library, 14 St James's Square, St James's, SW1Y 4LB
Martin (Adeel Akhtar) meets Carolyn in the library to report that he thinks Eve is too obsessed with Villanelle to be objective. Carolyn tries not to hear things which can make her life any more complex.

Banking Hall, 14 Cornhill, EC3V 3ND
Villanelle murders her target in the lift at the Banking Hall.

Darkhouse Restaurant and Bar, 16 Victory Parade, East Village, E20 1FS
Eve hides a microphone in some bread for Villanelle in this restaurant.

Season Three

Liverpool Street Underground Station, Liverpool Street, EC2M 1QT
Villanelle and Konstantin make their way down the train platform in a bid to escape but Konstantin has a heart attack. She asks him where he's hidden the money before he passes out and she is able to retrieve a piece of paper from his jacket pocket before she leaves him on the platform to die, jumping on a train. Eve arrives and gets a member of the public to call for an ambulance.

Rivoli Ballroom, 350 Brockley Road, SE4 2BY
Eve meets Villanelle here. Villanelle chose the venue as it was the location of the first kill she'd carried out in the UK; a high-ranking police officer who was a ballroom dancer. Eve tells Villanelle that Niko (Owen McDonnell) is in hospital because Dasha (Harriet Walter) stabbed him in the neck and had blamed it on Villanelle.

The Rivoli was originally built as a picture palace in 1913, and now is the only intact 1950s ballroom in London.

Scarfes Bar, Rosewood Hotel, 252 High Holborn, WC1V 7EN
www.scarfesbar.com

Carolyn is drinking in this bar before meeting with an acquaintance and gets some important information.

The bar is open for food and drink daily.

Tower Bridge, Tower Bridge Road, SE1 2UP
Villanelle and Eve meet on Tower Bridge in season three, episode eight.

The Clapton Hart, 231 Lower Clapton Road, Lower Clapton, E5 8EG
www.claptonhart.com

Kenny's Memorial was held here.

Tower Bridge, Tower Bridge Road, SE1 2UP

Serpentine Bridge, Hyde Park, W2 2UH
Mo Jafari (Raj Bajaj), Carolyn's assistant is at the Serpentine Bridge when he claims to have the link between Paul (Steve Pemberton) and the Twelve. This revelation was to cost him dearly.

Royal Albert Hall, Kensington Gore, South Kensington, SW7 2AP
www.royalalberthall.com

Carolyn meets Villanelle to get answers as to who killed Mo Jafari and her son.
   The Albert Hall was originally called the Royal Albert Hall of Arts and Science, in memory of Prince Albert. It was opened in March 1871 by Queen Victoria and has held thousands of concerts, and events since then. The Hall is open for guided tours or for ticketed shows.

Gilbert Scott Restaurant, St Pancras Renaissance Hotel, Euston Road, NW1 2AR
This was used for the Castle Stuart Hotel. Even though Villanelle is wearing tartan and affecting a Scottish accent to show it was in Scotland it was filmed at the base of the Grand Staircase in the St Pancras Hotel.

It was also used as the restaurant where following the morning briefing Carolyn tells them they don't deserve omelettes. Surely everyone deserves omelettes?

Seymour Leisure Centre, Seymour Place, W1H 5TJ
This was used for the Moscow Acrobatics Hall where Dasha misses a gymnastic landing.

Albert Hall Mansions, 31-48 Kensington Gore, SW7 2AW
The accountant who Konstantin visits was located in the Albert Hall Mansions.

Armourers Hall, 81 Coleman Street, EC2R 5BI
Villanelle meets with Hélène in this building and is surrounded by weapons.

Hamley's Toy Store, 188-196 Regent Street, W1B 5BT
Villanelle heads to Hamley's to get Eve a talking bear.

Floris, 89 Jermyn Street, St James's, SW1Y 6JH
Villanelle heads to Jermyn Street to buy a perfume that will make her smell powerful.

Savile Club, 69 Brook Street, W1K 4ER
Paul and Carolyn eat in the members' only restaurant at the Savile Club.

Greenfield Road, E1
Kenny (Sean Delaney) falls to his death from this building which is later declared a suicide.

Season Four

Saint Matthias Church, Wordsworth Road, N16 8DD
The season opens with Villanelle in church indicating she has found religion.

This church was designed by William Butterfield in 1853. It was badly damaged in 1941 when hit by a bomb but it was restored shortly afterwards.

St Pancras Station, Euston Road, N1C 4QL
Yusef (Robert Gilbert) and Eve start their journey to Paris in order to spy on Hélène (Camille Cottin).

London Aquatics Centre, E20 2ZQ
This was used for the filming of the Russian pool where Carolyn interrupts Vlad's (Laurence Possa) swim to talk about Hugo.

Averard Hotel, 16 Lancaster Gate, W2 3LH
Carolyn heads to Russia to continue her hunt for the Twelve. Her Russian accommodation was filmed at the Averard Hotel.

Averard Hotel, 16 Lancaster Gate, W2 3LH

The Grosvenor Pub, 76 Grosvenor Road, Pimlico, SW1V 3LA
www.thegrosvenorpub.business.site

Both Villanelle and Eve arrive at the Grosvenor in pursuit of the Twelve only to find Carolyn and Pam (Anjana Vasan) instead.

The Grosvenor is open daily for food and drink.

Cock and Bottle, 17 Needham Road, W11 2RP
www.cockandbottlew11.com

Eve and Fernanda (Monica Lopera) sit in the Cock and Bottle and talk about their exes.

The pub is open seven days a week for food and drink.

The Richmond Theatre, 1 Little Green, TW9 1QJ
www.atgtickets.com/venues/richmond-theatre

Hélène shows Eve the theatre her daddy had bought for her.

Designed by architect Frank Matcham the Richmond Theatre was opened in 1899. It has been an active theatre since it opened.

The Observatory, 64 Marchmont Street, WC1N 1AB
Eve waits for Villanelle and Billie to finish with AA and watches through the window.

However, in reality the café is not opposite the address so she couldn't have witnessed Villanelle dealing with Amber's (Shannon Tarbet) handler.

Sessions Art Club, Knotel, 24 Clerkenwell Green, EC1R 0NA
www.sessionsartsclub.com

Villanelle and Carolyn play truth or dare in this restaurant which is meant to be in Havana, Cuba while they wait for a member of the Twelve.

TV DRAMAS | 149

The Observatory, 64 Marchmont Street, WC1N 1AB

The Standard, 10th Floor, 10 Argyle Street, WC1H 8EG
Pam meets Hélène outside the hotel to talk about her family issues.

Eve follows Hélène into The Standard Bar where she is with another women. The shots were taken near the lifts on the tenth floor and the Decimo restaurant.

Lucky Voice Karaoke Bar, 84 Chancery Lane, WC2A 1DL
Eve and Yosef go to the karaoke bar in a bid to lift Eve's spirits, but she can't get into the swing of it due to thinking about everyone she has lost.

Luther (TV Series, 2010–2019)

Creator: Neil Cross

Series One (2010)

Titan House, 144 Southwark Street, SE1 0UP
This was the location for the Police Headquarters throughout the first season. In the first episode Luther (Idris Elba) makes a call to his estranged-wife, Zoe (Indira Varma) to ask about getting back together.

The Griffin, Leonard Street, EC2A 4RD
www.the-griffin.com

DCI John Luther and DCI Ian Reed (Steven Mackintosh) meet here for a drink in the first episode.

This pub is open daily for drinks.

97 Aldersgate Street, EC1A 4JP
Luther meets with Alice (Ruth Wilson) outside this building. She shows him the urn of her cremated dog and then invites him back to her place.

Blackfriars Road, SE1 9UD
Alice follows Luther from her flat, after he breaks in and steals the urn with the ashes of her dog, which also has the remains of the gun she used to kill her parents. He throws the urn over the bridge, saving the gun fragments.

64 Camberwell Grove, SE5 8RF
This is the house of Luther's wife and where he punches Mark North (Paul McGann), her new boyfriend in the face.

Charles Hocking House, 118 Bollo Bridge Road, W3 8SJ
Owen Lynch (Sam Spruell) shoots a police officer from the top of this building. Luther rushes to the scene with other officers as Owen continues shooting from the roof.

The area has been heavily developed since the filming.

HMP Wormwood Scrubs, 160 Du Cane Road, W12 0AN
Luther visits Terry Lynch (Sean Pertwee), Owen's dad in prison. He also conducts an interview for the TV outside the gates.

Southwark Bridge, EC4V 3BG
Luther meets Alice on the bridge for a pretty intense conversation. It is possible to see the Tate Modern in the background.

28 Lansdowne Gardens, SW8 2EG
Kirsten Ross (Catherine Hamilton) answers her door to a man claiming to be Detective Inspector Philip Hamilton, but he was really Lucien Burgess (Paul Rhys). He kidnaps her and puts her in the boot of his car.

Greenland Dock, Swedish Quay, SE16 7UF
Luther and his partner DS Justin Ripley (Warren Brown) go to a boat moored in Greenland Dock, to find Kirsten already dead in the freezer.

Liverpool Street Underground Station, Liverpool Street, EC2M 1QT
Throughout the first season many scenes were filmed in and around Liverpool Street Station.

Crowne Plaza London Shoreditch, 100 Shoreditch High Street, E1 6JQ
Lucien Burgess exits the hotel watched by DCI Ian Reed who is sitting in his car outside

The hotel has now closed but the building is still there.

Greenland Dock, Swedish Quay, SE16 7UF

Greenland Surrey Quays Pier, SE16 7TY
Luther and DSU Martin Schenk (Dermot Crowley) go for coffee to discuss Luther's suspension, but in the nick of time Mark North drops the allegations against him.

Westfield London, Ariel Way, W12 7GF
The art dealer James Carrodus (Thomas Lockyer) goes to meet his wife's kidnappers in Westfield. Filming was carried out at various locations throughout the shopping centre.

Lamb & Flag, 24 James Street, W1U 1EL
www.greeneking.co.uk/pubs/greater-london/lamb-and-flag

Greenland Surrey Quays Pier, SE16 7TY

After arresting the lady who was trying to retrieve the bag of diamonds from the bin she was bundled into a car outside the Lamb and Flag. Luther then speaks to the hostage taker on the phone.

The Lamb & Flag is open daily for food and drink.

St Giles Cripplegate, Fore Street, Barbican, EC2Y 8DA
Luther meets Alice in St Giles Church, Cripplegate to talk about Zoe, and before leaving he drops his wedding ring into the collection box.

This church is one of the few surviving medieval churches in London and was built in 1090. John Milton the author of *Paradise Lost* is buried here.

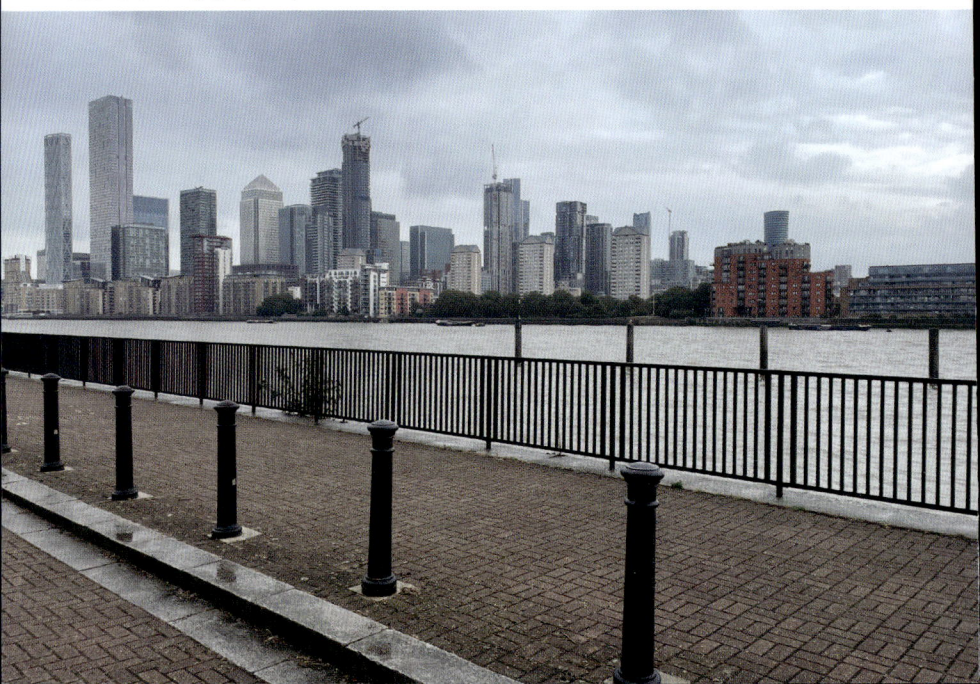

Westfield London, Ariel Way, W12 7GF

Renaissance London Heathrow Hotel, Bath Road, Hounslow, TW6 2AQ
Luther goes to the Renaissance Hotel to follow the kidnapper, Daniel Sugarman (Ross McCall) and the diamonds. DCI Ian Reed turns up and shoots him in the head before he has a chance to talk.

74 Wood Street, Barbican, EC2V 7WS
Luther enters the Barbican Centre via an escalator from this address.

Waterloo Station, Eurostar Platform (Platforms 20-22), SE1 8SR
Mark North stole the diamonds from his locker on the old Eurostar platform at Waterloo Station. Ian Reed tracks him down. Luther gets into a fight with Ian, which results in Luther being stabbed. Alice intervenes and points Ian's shotgun at him before shooting him.

The Eurostar ran here from November 1994 to November 2007.

Season Two

Grand Avenue, Smithfield Market, EC1A 9PS
Sadie Buckingham (unnamed actor) is seen walking down Grand Avenue shortly before her murder by a man wearing a Punch mask.

Godfrey Phillips, 112 Jerome Street, E1 6BX
Sadie's murder took place on Jerome Street. You can see the sign for 112, Godfrey Phillips in the background.

Petticoat Lane Market, Wentworth Street, E1 7TB
The second murder took place in Petticoat Lane Market in an alley between 24A and 26.

A market has been on this site since the seventeenth century.

Kent Court, 14 Kent Street, E2 8NU
After visiting Alice in prison Luther is filmed eating an apple and walking down Kent Street.

Haggerston Park, Yorkton Street, E2 8NH
Luther throws the apple core over the wall of the prison, which is picked up by Alice in the prison gardens. Later Luther returns to Old Street Magistrates' Court to meet Toby. This was filmed at Haggerston Park.

Courthouse Hotel Shoreditch, 337 Old Street, EC1V 9LL
Luther visits a video sex worker Jenny Jones (Aimee-Ffion Edwards) in what was Old Street Magistrates' Court which is now a hotel.

Clapton Vax Centre, 103 Lower Clapton Road, Lower Clapton, E5 0NP
DS Erin Gray (Nikki Amuka-Bird) takes Candice Calvert (Bryony Afferson) home after being questioned at the station. Her home was in the flat above what is now the Clapton Vax Centre.

24 Bateman's Row, EC2A 3HH
Luther's hand is nailed to the table by Toby Kent (David Dawson), one of Buba's henchmen at Caroline Jones' (Kierston Wareing) flat. This was filmed at Bateman's Row.

4 Princelet Street, E1 6QH
Luther and Jenny Jones have a chat outside the safe house on Princelet Street.

This building is a common location for film makers. It was built in 1723 and the red stucco was added in 1820.

4 Wilkes Street, E1 6QF
Luther and Mark North drive up to number 4 and let Jenny Jones out of the boot of their car. You can see the front of number 4 Princelet Street in the background.

Millennium Mills, West Silvertown 1, 23 Rayleigh Road, E16 1UR
Cameron Pell (Lee Ingleby) uses a bus to abduct the school children. He leaves their mobile phones as he abandons the bus and shifts the children to his van. He drives the van to Millennium Mills where he is confronted by Luther and DS Justin Ripley.

Lund Point, E15 2JN
Luther returns to his flat to find that Alice has escaped prison and is waiting in his flat. She asks him to run away with her. He refuses.

Arnold Circus, Calvert Avenue, Bethnal Green, E2 7JP
Robert Millberry (Steven Robertson) is seen sitting by the bandstand at Arnold Circus. He takes out his notebook and throws some dice before proceeding to walk down Calvert Avenue jumping on car roofs and setting off car alarms.

St Leonard's Church, 119 Shoreditch High Street, E1 6JN
Jenny Jones goes to St Leonard's Church, to meet with her mum.

It is thought this church could be the oldest continuous Christian site in England, with the earliest record being Roman from 46 CBE. The church currently on the site was built in 1740.

Liverpool Street Underground Station, Liverpool Street, EC2M 1QT
Millberry's identical twin, Nicholas enters Liverpool Street Station and lays out on the ground on the main concourse, with a hammer, knife, small baseball bat and a water pistol loaded with acid. He then throws a dice before rampaging through the station attacking pedestrians.

Blake Tower, 2 Fann Street, EC2Y 8AF
Luther goes to Robert Millberry's which was opposite the Shakespeare's Pub.

Hijingo Bingo, 90 Worship Street, EC2A 2BA
Nicholas Millberry enters a coffee shop to check his emails. The police track his laptop to the location. He reveals he is wearing a bomb vest.

44 Moorfields, EC2Y 9AL
Millberry then walks off towards the square.

5–6 Moorgate, EC2M 6XB
Luther confronts Nicholas outside number 5–6 Moorgate, with the tube station in the background. Luther covers himself in petrol and gives a lighter to Nicholas.

90–98 Sclater Street, E1 6HR
Luther and Molly get an ice cream from a van on Sclater Street.

Season Four

Stafford Cripps Estate, Islington, SW6 7RX

In season four a top floor flat was blown up at Stafford Cripps Estate. This was however done via CGI in post-production or it may have startled the residents.

Season Five

Rivoli Ballroom, 350 Brockley Road, SE4 2BY

In season five, Luther was tied up and threatened by a gang of gun-wielding thugs in this ballroom.

The Rivoli was originally built as a picture palace in 1913, and now is the only intact 1950s ballroom in London.

Poirot – The Veiled Lady (1990)

Dir. Edward Bennett

Earlsfield Police Station, 522 Garratt Lane, SW17 0NZ

The shots of the police station were taken here.

At the time of filming this was Earlsfield Police Station but it closed in 2001.

Burlington Arcade, 51 Piccadilly, W1J 0QJ

This is where the jewel robbery took place.

Poirot – The Jewel Robbery at the Grand Metropole (1993)

Dir. Ken Grieve

Marylebone Station, Melcombe Place, NW1 6JJ

This was used in place of Eastbourne train station where Poirot (David Suchet) and Captain Hastings (Hugh Fraser) leave London for Poirot's health, and where he later meets Miss Lemon (Pauline Moran).

New Wimbledon Theatre, 93 The Broadway, SW19 1QG

www.atgtickets.com/venues/new-wimbledon-theatre

The foyer was used for the scene where Poirot and Hastings go to the theatre on the opening night of *Pearls Before Swine*. He is accosted on the stairs by a gaggle of journalists.

This Grade II listed theatre calls itself the home of London pantomime and was designed by Cecil Aubrey Massey and Roy Young and is rumoured to have included Turkish baths in the basement. It opened on Boxing Day 1910 with the pantomime, *Jack and Jill*.

Poirot – The Clocks (2009)

Dir. Charles Palmer

Woburn Walk, WC1H 0JL

The Cavendish Secretarial Bureau was located on this street.

Thornhill Crescent, N1 1BL
Wilbrahim Crescent in the show was filmed on location on Thornhill Crescent.

Poirot – Elephants Can Remember (TV Series, 2014)

Dir. John Strickland

Sheraton Grand London, Park Lane, 51-53 Brick Street, W1J 7DH
Ariadne Oliver (Zoe Wannamaker) is declared crime writer of the year at an event held at this hotel and is approached about the deaths of her goddaughter's parents.

Florin Court, 6-9 Charterhouse Square, Barbican, EC1M 6EU

Florin Court, 6-9 Charterhouse Square, Barbican, EC1M 6EU
This 1930s building was meant to be Whitehaven Mansions, where Poirot (David Suchet) lived, and was used in many of the episodes of this TV programme.

Dean Rees House, Queen Mary University of London, Charterhouse Square, EC1M 6BQ
The exterior shots of the Willoughby Institute, where the body of Professor Willoughby was found in the bath were filmed here.

Charterhouse Mews, EC1M 6AH

The Charterhouse, Charterhouse Square, EC1M 6AM

Charterhouse Mews, EC1M 6AH
The wigmakers shop, Eugene and Rosenthal (which had stopped selling wigs and changed to a hairdressers) was located down this mews.

The entrance to the mews is next to 22 Charterhouse Square.

The Charterhouse, Charterhouse Square
The piano recital took place here where Poirot spoke with Celia Ravenscroft (Vanessa Kirby).

Poirot: The Big Four (2013)

Dir. Peter Lyndon

Kensal Green Cemetery, Harrow Road, W10 4RA
The episode opens with the funeral of Hercule Poirot (David Suchet) which is held at Kensal Green Cemetery. The shots are artistic through the gravestones making pinpointing the exact location difficult.

Maitland Chambers, 7 Stone Buildings, WC2A 3S2
The exterior shot of Mr Ingles' (Nicholas Day) offices was filmed at Lincoln's Inn. The interior shots of the stairs were filmed in Syon House in Brentford.

Richmond Theatre, 1 Little Green, Richmond, TW9 1QJ
www.atgtickets.com/venues/richmond-theatre

The exterior of the theatre where Flossie Monroe (Sarah Parish) was performing were filmed at Richmond Theatre.

Designed by architect Frank Matcham the Richmond Theatre was opened in 1899. It has been an active theatre since it opened.

Undercroft, Lincoln's Inn, Treasury Office, WC2A 3TL
The journalist, Mr Tysoe (Tom Brooke) meets Poirot here about the skeletons in the cupboard and how Abe Ryland (James Carroll Jordon) made his money in the arms trade as well as introducing the Big Four.

This was also the location where the homeless man was murdered by being stabbed and there was a note in his pocket for the journalist.

4 New Square, WC2A 3RJ

Poirot heads into the basement flat of number 41, just before the building explodes.

Florin Court, 6-9 Charterhouse Square, Barbican, EC1M 6EU

This 1930s building was meant to be Whitehaven Mansions, where Poirot lived, and was used in many of the episodes of this TV programme.

Noël Coward Theatre, 85-88 St Martin's Lane, WC2N 4AP

www.noelcowardtheatre.co.uk

This was used for the Methuselah Theatre entrance where Flossie goes for the audition which never happens. Instead she is captured and tied to a chair and subjected to a 'performance' by the Big Four.

The theatre was first opened in 1902 and Noël Coward made his debut at the theatre in his own play *I'll Leave It to You*. It has been an active theatre since it opened.

Hackney Empire, 291 Mare Street, E8 1EJ

The internal shots of the theatre where the big reveal was made by Poirot were filmed inside the Hackney Empire.

The Hackney Empire was designed by architect Frank Matcham and opened in 1901 as an entertainment space starting as a music hall with

4 New Square, WC2A 3RJ

performers including Julie Andrews and Charlie Chaplin. In 1956 it was a television studio, until it was opened as a bingo hall in 1963. In the 1980s it was saved from being demolished and turned into a car park. It is now an arts centre.

Sherlock (TV Series, 2010–2017)

Creators: Mark Gatiss, Steven Moffat

Russell Square Gardens, WC1H 0XG
Dr John Watson (Martin Freeman) meets Mike Stamford (David Nellist) at Russell Square and talks about how hard it'd been since he left the front. Stamford suggests cheap lodgings at 221b Baker Street.

187 North Gower Street, NW1 2NJ
Throughout all four seasons this is where Sherlock Holmes (Benedict Cumberbatch) and John Watson live. In the books it was 221b Baker Street but in the TV series it is above Speedy's Café. In the pilot the café was renamed 'Mrs Hudson's Snax' but remained as Speedy's throughout the show. They provide themed dishes to keep the Sherlock fans happy.

St Bartholomew's Hospital, W Smithfield, EC1A 7BE
St Bart's Hospital was another regular location throughout all seasons as it is where Molly Hooper (Louise Brealey) works, and where Watson is studying. At the end of season two Holmes leaps from the top of the building as he fakes his own death.

The hospital is the oldest working hospital in the UK and has been on the site since 1123. There is a small museum on the site telling the history of the hospital.

Oxo Tower Foreshore, SE1 9PH
This was where the body of the gallery security guard was found washed up in season one. If you want to go down to the shore check tide times and be careful.

Old Bailey, EC4M 7EH
The exterior of the Old Bailey was used throughout the first two seasons and it was the site of the trial of Jim Moriarty (Andrew Scott).

New Scotland Yard, Victoria Embankment, SW1A 2JL
In season one, inspectors Lestrade (Rupert Graves) and Dimmock (Paul Chequer) and Sergeant Donovan (Vinette Robinson) work alongside Holmes and Watson to solve the crime here at New Scotland Yard.

Feng Shui Inn, 6 Gerrard Street, W1D 5PG
In season one, Holmes and Watson are investigating in China Town and can be seen passing the Feng Shui Inn and the Lucky Cat.

New Scotland Yard, Victoria Embankment, SW1A 2JL

Tapas Brindisa Soho, 46 Broadwick Street, W1F 7AE

In season one, Holmes and Watson sat in a booth in this restaurant where they discussed Watson's injury.

The restaurant has been refurbished but the booth is the same and has a picture of Sherlock over it.

10 Carlton House Terrace, St James's, SW1Y 5ED

Sherlock's brother, Mycroft (Mark Gatliss) was a member of the Diogenes Club, which was filmed here. Watson causes a scene when he speaks loudly inside the club despite the no talking rule.

South Bank Skate Park, 337–338 Belvedere Road, SE1 8XT

In season two, graffiti artist Raz (Jack Bence) shows Holmes and Watson some cryptic symbols which have appeared at the skate park.

This area is an unofficial skateboarding and street art venue on the Southbank.

Battersea Power Station, Circus Road West, Nine Elms, SW11 8AL

Sherlock meets Irene Adler (Lara Pulver) here in season two. She is one of Holmes's only weaknesses.

At the time of filming the Power Station was derelict and has since been redeveloped into a shopping centre although it has maintained a lot of its original features.

44 Eaton Square, SW1W 9BD

This was the home of Irene Adler.

Boscobel Place, SW1W 9PE

This was the site of a massive row between Holmes and Watson when Holmes declared he needed a disguise.

Tower of London, EC3N 4AB

Moriarty does a reconnaissance trip as a tourist around the Tower of London to see where the crown jewels are positioned.

The Landmark London, 222 Marylebone Road, NW1 6JQ

The exterior shots for the Reunion restaurant were filmed at The Landmark London, and the interior shots were at The Daffodil in Cheltenham. At the end of season two Holmes and Watson are reunited.

Whitfield Street, W1T 4EU

In season two, a rather hair-raising taxi journey finished on Whitfield Street.

American International Church, 79a Tottenham Court Road, W1T 4TD
In season two, the sniper takes aim from the second-floor window on the stairwell of the American Church in London.

55 Whitehall, SW1A 2HP
Holmes stands on top of this building in season three to view the city.

Westminster Underground Station, Bridge Street, SW1A 2JR
In season three, Holmes and Watson enter the station through the ticket hall and break through a maintenance barrier into the depths of the tube system.

Aldwych Underground, 3 India Place, WC2B 4NA
www.ltmuseum.co.uk/hidden-london

Holmes appears on a disused platform of what is named Sumatra Road (a fictional station) – this was filmed at Aldwych Station.

Aldwych Station was officially closed in 1994, as it was not cost effective to renovate it. However, it has been used as a filming location since then and is occasionally opened to the public for specialist tours run by the London Transport Museum.

23-24 Leinster Gardens, W2 3AN
Holmes meets with Watson's wife Mary (Amanda Abbington) and a secret assassin here in season three. Watson sees her face projected onto the frontage of these buildings.

You will notice this building has two doors, no letter boxes and false windows and is actually a façade to hide the vent for the train station behind. It was built when the trains were steam and it was needed to keep the underground clear. The walls are approximately 5 metres thick.

Top Boy (TV Series, 2011–2023)

Creator: Ronan Bennett

Whipps Cross University Hospital, Whipps Cross Road, E11 1NR
This hospital appeared across the seasons in *Top Boy*, including when Lisa (Sharon Duncan-Brewster) is hospitalised over her mental health and when Dushane's mother (Pat Hill) is admitted as her heath deteriorates as well as the harrowing fight scene.

Samuda Estate, Manchester Road, E14 3HA
In seasons three and four, Summerhouse Estate, the centre of the show was filmed at the Samuda Estate on the Isle of Dogs.

Dushane (Ashley Walters) and Sully (Kane 'Kano' Robinson) both live here and it is where all the drug gangs operate from. The original inspiration for Summerhouse Estate was the De Beauvoir Estate in Hackney.

Number One Café, 36-38 Well Street, E9 7PX
Dushane and Sully spend a lot of time in this café shooting the breeze but also arranging their ropey business deals.

Old English Garden, Victoria Park, Grove Road, E3 5TB
The three orphaned brothers Jamie (Michael Ward), Stefan (Araloyin Oshunremi) and Aaron (Hope Ikpoku Jr) find solace on a bench in the Old English Garden. In season two it's where they go to remember their parents but also where Stefan goes to feel close to Jamie.

The garden was originally planted in 1916, but after being neglected was restored in 2012.

Ridley Road Market, St Mark's Rise, E8 2PD
Much of the street dealing across the seasons took place at Ridley Road Market. The market is governed by Jaq (Jasmin Jobson) who has little sympathy for the effects drugs are having on the local people.

Ridley Road Market started with approximately 20 stalls in the 1880s and now has more than 150 today. The market is open daily from 9.30am to 4pm.

Gee Street, EC1V
As east London is slowly gentrified Dushane moves into a flat in Gee Street.

Kiki's Nail Salon, Freemasons Road, E16
Shelley's (Little Simz) nail bar was filmed at Kiki's on Freemasons Road.

Valmont Club, 266 Fulham Road, SW10 9EL
Many of the characters met at this club to talk business.

At the time of filming the club was serviced offices but had closed by 2018 and now stands derelict.

Ark Walworth Academy, Shorncliffe Road, SE1 5UJ
All the school scenes in the show were filmed here. To add to the authenticity, often the extras were pupils from the school.

Blackfriars Crown Court, 1-15 Pocock Street, SE1 0BT
In season four, the legal scenes were filmed at Blackfriars Crown Court, where it was revealed the Nittys were working as undercover police.

By 2020 this courthouse had closed permanently and currently stands empty.

Darkhorse, 16 Victory Parade, East Village, E20 1FS
Lizzie (Lisa Dwan) has dinner with Jeffrey (Shaun Dingwall) when she receives a call from Emilio (Hugo Silva) in Spain.

Prospect of Whitby, 57 Wapping Wall, E1W 3SH
www.greeneking.co.uk/pubs/greater-london/prospect-of-whitby

By entering a passageway alongside this pub you will come across a small beach which appeared in season four.

As you're here you could pop into the pub too, which was built in 1520 and is one of the oldest riverside pubs. The pub is open daily for food and drink.

You

Dir. Penn Badgley

(Season Four 2022)

Establishing Shots
In order to set the scene there are numerous establishing shots of London, to make it clear to viewers where it was filmed.

- Tower Bridge, Tower Bridge Road, SE1 2UP
- 150 Piccadilly, St James's, W1J 9BR
- Regents Street, SW1Y 4PE
- Big Ben, 67 Bridge Street, SW1A 2PW

Christ Church Spitalfields, Commercial Street, E1 6LY
Joe Goldberg (Penn Badgley) leaves the university, and it is possible to see Christ Church Spitalfields in the background of the shot.

Christ Church opened in 1729, as part of a drive to build fifty new churches proposed in 1711. They offer guided tours but these must be booked in advance.

Lincoln's Inn, 11 New Square, WC2A 3QB
The Darcy College Library is filmed within the Honourable Society of Lincoln's Inn.

10 Kynance Mews, SW7 4QP
Joe Goldberg lives in Kynance Mews and there are shots of him walking past the sign for Lanceston Place, (W8 5RL) before he turns into Kynance Mews. The close-up shots of the mews were filmed in a studio.

St Pancras, Euston Road, N1C 4QP
This is where Joe steals Marienne's (Tati Gabrielle) necklace. He walks down a narrow alley which is red brick lined onto the upper floor of the station, where he bumps into her knocking her over.

Four Seasons Hotel, 10 Trinity Square, EC3N 4AJ
The rich heiress, Phoebe (Tilly Keeper), lives in flat in this building. Both the interior and exterior shots were filmed here.

69 Cornwall Gardens, SW7 4BA
The exterior shots of Kate's (Charlotte Ritchie) flat were filmed here. The interior shots were filmed in a set.

Gloucester Road Underground Ltd, Gloucester Road, South Kensington, SW7 4SF
As Joe travels around London there are some great shots of this tube station.

Fabric Nightclub, 77A Charterhouse Street, EC1M 6HJ

The interior shots of the club scenes were filmed at Fabric nightclub.

Old Billingsgate, 1 Old Billingsgate Walk (Riverside), 16 Lower Thames Street, EC3R 6DX

The gallery where Kate hosts Simon Soo's (Aiden Cheng) art show was filmed here. Old Billingsgate is an event space but was once a famous fish market which closed in 1982. Joe is seen sitting on the bench to the right of the building looking on.

St Bartholemew the Great, West Smithfield, Barbican, EC1A 9DS

This church was where the memorial/funeral was held for Simon Soo, and also where the 'Eat the Rich' protestors were standing.

St Bartholomew the Great was founded as an Augustinian priory in 1123.

The Builder's Arms, 1 Kensington Court Place, W8 5BJ

www.thebuildersarmskensington.co.uk

Joe follows Kate to this pub after the funeral.

This pub is open daily for food and drink and shows major sporting events.

The Bargehouse, Oxo Tower Wharf, Barge House Street, SE1 9PH

This exhibition space in the Oxo Tower is used in numerous episodes starting with the first episode when, Joe chases

Fabric Nightclub, 77A Charterhouse Street, EC1M 6HJ

The Bargehouse, Oxo Tower Wharf, Barge House Street, SE1 9PH

The Bargehouse, Oxo Tower Wharf, Barge House Street, SE1 9PH (door 16)

Marienne through the door at the end on the left marked with a number 16.

Kate's gallery is also filmed in this building.

Seething Lane Garden, Seething Lane, EC3N 4AT

The little garden, which includes a formal lawn, seating and a pergola, is a little pocket of peace among the hustle and bustle of London. This is where Joe starts spying on the Nigerian princes, Blessing (Oziomo Whenu) and Gemma (Eve Austin).

The Approach Tavern, 47 Approach Road, E2 9LY

www.theapproachtavern.co.uk

Joe meets Connie (Dario Coates) here to see if he can frame him for the murders. Connie is lamenting the pointlessness of his life now he is unable to take cocaine.

Globe Tavern, 8 Bedale Street, Borough Market, SE1 9AL

www.theglobeboroughmarket.com

Joe and Kate walk along Bedale Street, towards the Globe Tavern whilst they are eating chips and he suggests she meets her father rather than running away.

This pub is open daily for drinks only.

Royal Victoria Dock, Footbridge, Gallions Point Marina, E16 1XL

This is where the scene is shot where Joe decides to kill himself by jumping off the bridge taking his alter-ego with him.

9
RELATED SITES

Cinema Museum, The Master's House, 2 Dugard Way (off Renfrew Road), SE11 4TH
www.cinemamuseum.org.uk

This little museum is an eclectic collection of memorabilia of the history of British cinema including cinema furniture and projectors, to staff uniforms and movie posters. You can also sit yourself in the cinema and watch clips from early cinema.

You have to book a tour and the guides are clearly passionate about movies and the cinema.

Agatha Christie Memorial, Cranbourn Street, WC2H 7AB
This memorial statue was designed by Ben Twiston-Davies and was unveiled in 2012. In addition to Christie being the queen of crime, this memorial was designed to celebrate her play *The Mousetrap* which is the world's longest-running show. It opened at the Ambassador's Theatre in November 1952, and has been playing at St Martin's Theatre since 1974.

47-48 Campden Street, W8 7ET
Agatha Christie lived here in 1930-1934 when she was starting her mystery novel writing career.

58 Sheffield Terrace, Holland Park, W8 7NA
Agatha Christie wrote *Murder on the Orient Express* (1934) and *Death on the Nile* (1937) when she lived at Sheffield Terrace. She lived here with her archaeologist husband Max Malloran between 1934 and 1941. There is a Blue Plaque on the building to commemorate this.

Sherlock Holmes Pub, 10 Northumberland Street, WC2N 5DB
www.greeneking.co.uk/pubs/greater-london/sherlock-holmes

This is a Sherlock Holmes themed pub, which had a small museum with Holmes memorabilia and the upstairs restaurant is decorated to look like his sitting room.

This pub is open seven days a week for food and drink.

Sherlock Holmes Statue, Baker Street Underground Station, Marylebone Road, NW1 5LJ

Sherlock Holmes Museum, 221b Baker Street, NW1 6XE

Sherlock Holmes Statue, Baker Street Underground Station, Marylebone Road, NW1 5LJ

This statue was created by sculptor John Doubleday and was erected in 1999. It was meant to be installed near 221b Baker Street but with no suitable address it was installed here just a short distance away.

Sherlock Holmes Museum, 221b Baker Street, NW1 6XE

www.sherlock-holmes.co.uk

A small museum dedicated to all things Sherlock Holmes based in what is meant to be the fictional address. The house dates back to 1815 and has been decorated to represent the rooms that Holmes would have rented between 1881 and 1904.

There are guides in costume throughout the museum to help guide your experience.

10
PUB CRAWL

A staple of British culture, and indeed the London-based crime movie is the pub, and therefore a pub crawl is a must. These are organised by rough areas of London (north, south, east and west) but we wouldn't recommend doing the whole lot in a day. Drink responsibly peeps.

North

The Stag's Head, Orsman Road, N1 5RA
www.stagsheadhoxton.com

In *Legend* Ronnie (Tom Hardy) falls out with Leslie and glasses him in the face here. Ronnie was worried that Leslie knew too many 'things' about the Krays and shouldn't be trusted.

The Stag's Head is open daily for drinks and food and also have regular live music.

The Bacchus, 177 Hoxton Street, N1 6PJ
This pub represented the Blind Beggar where Ronnie Kray (Gary Kemp) killed George Cornell (Steven Berkoff) by shooting him in the face in *The Krays*. This bar was refurbished into the Superheroes Bar, a comic book inspired bar serving drinks and afternoon tea and has now re-emerged as the Bacchus Bar.

8-9 Hoxton Square, N1 6NU
www.happinessforgets.com

Dil (Jay Davidson) in *The Crying Game* lived at number 8–9 Hoxton Square and we see Fergus (Stephen Rea) watching him.

The site is now a cocktail bar called Happiness Forgets and is open every evening.

The Salisbury, 1 Green Lanes, Haringey Ladder, N4 1JX
www.thesalisburyhotelpub.co.uk

In *The Long Good Friday*, this was the location of Fagan's Irish Pub where Colin (Paul Freeman) hits on the doomed Irish lad (Kevin McNally).

The Salisbury currently offer food and drink.

Doyles Tavern, 359 Pentonville Road, N7 9DQ

www.doylestavern.co.uk

In *London Boulevard* Billy (Ben Chaplin) waits for Mitchel opposite the prison outside the pub.

This pub is open daily for drinks as well as showing all major sporting events.

South

Globe Tavern, 8 Bedale Street, Borough Market, SE1 9AL

www.theglobeboroughmarket.com

In season four of *You* Joe (Penn Badgley) and Kate (Charlotte Ritchie) walk along Bedale Street, towards the Globe Tavern whilst they are eating chips and he suggests she meets her father rather than running away.

This pub is open daily for drinks only.

Anchor Tavern, 34 Park Street, SE1 9EF

In *Mission: Impossible* Ethan (Tom Cruise) relaxes on the terrace of the Anchor Tavern with Luther Stickell (Ving Rhames).

The Anchor was built in 1615, and boasts Samuel Pepys watching the Great Fire of London on the north side of the river from here in 1666.

Spit and Sawdust, 21 Bartholomew Street, SE1 4AL

www.spitandsawdust.pub

Globe Tavern, 8 Bedale Street, Borough Market, SE1 9AL

In *London Boulevard*, Mitchel (Colin Farrell) enters the Spit and Sawdust and beats Billy Norton (Ben Chaplin) in order to extract information about how Gant (Ray Winstone) knows so much about him. He then steals the money Billy had collected for Gant.

The Spit and Sawdust is open daily for food and drink.

Black Prince, 6 Black Prince Road, Kennington, SE11 6HS
www.theblackprincepub.co.uk

In the *Kingsman* Eggsy (Taron Egerton) and his friends go to the pub and steal the keys of the guy they had an argument with. They then do donuts outside the pub to mock him. Throughout the film this is where all the pub scenes are shot, including the classic where Harry Hart (Colin Firth) takes out all five of the gang who tried to start a fight with Eggsy.

This pub is open daily for food and drink.

Hanover Arms, 326 Kennington Park Road, SE11 4PP
In *London Boulevard* Mitchel (Colin Farrell) meets Danny (Stephen Graham) and Billy (Ben Chaplin) in the pub for his coming out of prison party.

They are open daily for food and drinks.

Jolly Gardeners, 49-51 Black Prince Road, SE11 6AB
www.thejollygardeners.co.uk

In *Snatch* Bullet-Tooth Tony (Vinnie Jones) is confronted by Sol (Lennie James) and his gang at the Drowning Trout pub.

The pub was originally the Jolly Gardeners, then it was briefly a German gastropub called Zeitgeist. It has since reopened as a community pub, once more called the Jolly Gardeners which is open daily for food and drink.

The Ivy House, 40 Stuart Road, Peckham, SE15 3BE
www.ivyhousenunhead.co.uk

In *Legend* Reggie (Tom Hardy) takes Frances (Emily Browning) to The Double R Club in a bid to impress her and she spots Joan Collins in the crowd. They have their first kiss here.

The Ivy House is London's first co-operatively owned pub. It is Grade II listed and boasts a number of original 1930s features. They are open daily for food and drink.

The Ship & Whale, 2 Gulliver Street, SE16 7LT

The Ship & Whale, 2 Gulliver Street, SE16 7LT
www.shipandwhale.co.uk

In *The Gold* Brian Boyce meets Edwyn Cooper here, and Gordon Parry (Sean Harris) tells them the gold is behind the bar. He asks Cooper to help him get it, before they do a runner out the back of the pub.

The pub was first built in 1767 but the present building is dated to the 1880s. They are open every evening for food and drinks and all day on Saturday and Sunday.

The Albert, 52 Victoria Street, SW1H 0NP
www.greeneking.co.uk/pubs/greater-london/albert

In season one of *Killing Eve* Bill (David Haig) and Eve (Sandra Oh) talk to Frank (Darren Boyd) about the CCTV footage.

The pub is open daily for food and drink.

The Grosvenor Pub, 76 Grosvenor Road, Pimlico, SW1V 3LA
www.thegrosvenorpub.business.site

In season four of *Killing Eve* both Villanelle (Jodie Comer) and Eve arrive at The Grosvenor in pursuit of the Twelve only to find Carolyn (Fiona Shaw) and Pam (Anjana Vasan) instead.

The Grosvenor is open daily for food and drink.

Harwood Arms, Walham Grove, SW6 1QJ
www.harwoodarms.com

In *Football Factory* Bill (Dudley Sutton) and Albert (John Junkin) catch the taxi outside the pub to take them to the dancing venue.

This upmarket pub is open daily for lunch and dinner and may require a reservation.

East

Ten Bells Pub, 84 Commercial Street, E1 6LY
www.tenbells.com

This was the local pub of many of the killer's victims in *The Crying Game*.

This pub is open daily for beer, wine and cocktails.

Turner's Old Star, 14 Watts Street, E1W 2QG
www.turnersoldstar.co.uk

In *Legend* Turner's Old Star was used for the Pig and Whistle where a discussion between the Krays and Richardsons quickly descends into a punch up.

Ronnie (Tom Hardy) feigns leaving as he is disappointed the Richardsons brought 'rolling pins' rather than guns. He returns with two hammers.

The pub used to be owned by J.W. Turner the painter. The Old Star is open daily for drinks.

Ten Bells Pub, 84 Commercial Street, E1 6QQ

Prospect of Whitby, 57 Wapping Wall, E1W 3SH
www.greeneking.co.uk/pubs/greater-london/prospect-of-whitby

By entering a passageway alongside this pub you will come across a small beach which appeared in season four of *Top Boy*.

As you're here you could pop into the pub too, which was built in 1520 and is one of the oldest riverside pubs. The pub is open daily for food and drink.

The Royal Oak, 73 Columbia Road, E2 7RG
www.royaloakbethnalgreen.co.uk

In *Legend* Ronnie (Tom Hardy) kills George Cornell (Shane Attwooll) in the Blind Beggar for calling him a 'Fat poof'. This was filmed in The Royal Oak on Columbia Road.

The pub was also used in *The Krays* where the twins (Gary and Martin Kemp) and their gang enter The Royal Oak pub and pepper the entire bar with bullets

The pub is open daily for food and drinks.

The Approach Tavern, 47 Approach Road, E2 9LY
www.theapproachtavern.co.uk

In season four of *You* Joe meets Connie (Dario Coates) here to see if he can frame him for the murders. Connie is lamenting the pointlessness of his life now he is unable to take cocaine.

This pub is open daily for food and drinks.

Clapton Hart Pub, 231 Lower Clapton Road, E5 8EG
www.claptonhart.com

In season one of *Killing Eve* Bill's (David Haig) wake was held in this pub, and then in season three, Kenny's memorial was also held here.

They are open daily for food and drink.

Cat and Mutton Pub, 76 Broadway Market, E8 4RA
www.catandmutton.com

At the beginning of *Buster*, Buster Edwards (Phil Collins) walks past this pub after stealing a suit.

This pub was established in 1729 and is open daily for food and drink.

Northcote Arms, 110 Grove Green Road, E11 4EL
www.northcotee11.com

In *Vendetta* Jimmy (Danny Dyer) goes here when he returns to London following the murder of his parents. He questions Terry (Ben Shockley) about what he saw and finds out Terry was the one who had called the fire service but still watched the house burn.

The pub is open every day for food and drink but check for specific times.

Birkbeck Tavern, 45 Langthorne Road, E11 4HL
www.thebirkbecktavern.co.uk

In *Vendetta* Detective Spencer Holland (Alistair Petrie) went to the pub to get Terry's (Ben Shockley) CCTV showing Jimmy putting the body in the back of the car.

The Birkbeck Tavern is open daily for drinks.

The Waterman's Arms, 1 Glenaffric Avenue, E14 3BW
www.thewatermansarms.co.uk

The interior shots of the 'Governor General Pub' in *The Long Good Friday* were filmed at the Waterman's Arms. It is here that Harold (Bob Hoskins), finds Billy (Nick Stringer) and tells him to walk to the car.

The pub is open daily for food and drink.

The Railway Tavern Hotel, 131 Angel Lane, E15 1DB
www.the-railway-tavern-hotel.business.site

In *The Hatton Garden Job* Brian Reader (Larry Lamb), Danny Jones (Phil Daniels) and 'XXX' (Matthew Goode) meet to discuss the Hatton Garden job and who else will be involved.

This pub is open daily for drinks and 24 hours on Friday and Saturday.

Shoreditch Balls, 333 Old Street, EC1V 9LE
www.shoreditchballs.com

The interior shots of the 'Metro Bar', where Dil (Jaye Davidson) sings in *The Crying Game*, was filmed here. At the time of filming it was the London Apprentice. Today it is Shoreditch Balls and combines food, drink and mini-golf.

Ye Olde Mitre Tavern, 1 Ely Court, EC1N 6SJ
www.yeoldemitreholborn.co.uk

Doug 'the Head's' (Mike Reid) local was the Mitre Tavern. In one scene Guy Ritchie, the director, makes an appearance as 'man reading newspaper'.

The pub is unusually officially part of the county of Cambridgeshire, due to being built in 1547 for the servants of the palace of the Bishops of Ely, Cambridgeshire. Although in London, officially it isn't and it is rumoured that the Metropolitan Police can't enter without permission. Also the pub boasts an old wooden cherry tree stump and it is believed Elizabeth I danced around it.

Ye Olde Mitre is open Monday to Friday for food and drink and is closed at the weekend.

Ye Olde Mitre Tavern, 1 Ely Court, EC1N 6SJ

The Griffin, Leonard Street, EC2A 4RD
www.the-griffin.com

DCI John Luther (Idris Elba) and DCI Ian Reed (Steven Mackintosh) meet here for a drink in the opening scene of the first season of the TV series of *Luther*.

This pub is open daily for drinks.

The Grapes, 14 Lime Street, EC3M 7AN

In *Johnny English* The hearse escapes through the streets of London and is seen driving past The Grapes Pub.

The pub is open Monday to Friday for food and drink but is closed at weekends.

New Moon Pub, Leadenhall Market, Gracechurch Street, EC3V 1LT
www.newmoonleadenhall.com

In *Green Street* Matt (Elijah Wood) speaks with his dad (Henry Goodman) when he finds out he was thrown out of Harvard. They were sitting outside the New Moon Pub before walking towards the Gracechurch Street entrance.

They are open Monday to Saturday for food and drinks. They are closed on Sunday.

The Blackfriar, 174 Queen Victoria Street, EC4V 4EG
www.nicholsonspubs.co.uk/restaurants/london/theblackfriarblackfriarslondon

In *Men In Black International* Agent H (Chris Hemsworth) enters the London MIB HQ via the typewriter shop, although in reality this is actually a pub.

The Blackfriar was built in 1875 on the site of a Dominican Priory. It was then re-designed by H. Fuller-Clark and Henry Poole in 1905 and Poole's original carved friars are still scattered around the bar.

They are open daily for food and drink, and show all major sport fixtures.

West

Lamb & Flag, 24 James Street, W1U 1EL
www.greeneking.co.uk/pubs/greater-london/lamb-and-flag

In *Luther* season one after arresting a lady who was trying to retrieve a bag of diamonds from a bin she was bundled into a car outside the Lamb and Flag. Luther then speaks to the hostage taker on the phone.

The Lamb and Flag is open daily for food and drink.

Newman Arms, 23 Rathbone Street, W1 1NG
www.thenewmanarms.co.uk

In *Peeping Tom* the first of Mark Lewis's (Karlheinz Böhm) victims was picked up just off Oxford Street and taken to her room above the Newman Arms pub where her murder is filmed.

They offer food and drink but are closed on Sundays.

The Toucan, 19 Carlisle Street, W1D 3BY
www.thetoucansoho.co.uk

In *Last Night in Soho* Ellie (Thomasin McKenzie) works in The Toucan pub on Carlisle Street. The filming was done both inside and outside the pub.

The Toucan is an Irish pub which specialises in Guinness and is open every afternoon for drinks but is closed on Sunday.

The Blue Posts, Berwick Street, W1F 0QA
www.theblueposts.net

In one of the establishing shots of Carnaby Street in *Last Night in Soho* the Blue Posts pub is visible on Berwick Street.

They are open every day for drinks.

Serpentine Bar and Kitchen, Hyde Park, Serpentine Road, W2 2UH
www.benugo.com/sites/restaurants/serpentine-bar-kitchen

In *Robbery* Inspector George Langdon (James Booth) meets with an informant in the Serpentine Restaurant in Hyde Park.

They are open daily for food and drink.

The Toucan, 19 Carlisle Street, W1D 3BY

The Blue Posts, Berwick Street, W1F 0QA

The Viaduct, 221 Uxbridge Road, W7 3TD
www.viaduct-hanwell.co.uk

In *King of Thieves* Kenny (Tom Courtenay) meets Terry Perkins (Jim Broadbent) and Danny Jones (Ray Winstone) at the King's Arms which in reality is the Viaduct.

They are open daily for food and drink.

The Builder's Arms, 1 Kensington Court Place, W8 5BJ
www.thebuildersarmskensington.co.uk
In season four of *You* Joe (Penn Badgley) follows Kate (Charlotte Ritchie) to this pub after the funeral.

This pub is open daily for food and drink and shows major sporting events.

Cock and Bottle, 17 Needham Road, W11 2RP
www.cockandbottlew11.com

In season four of *Killing Eve*, Eve (Sandra Oh) and Fernanda (Monica Lopera) sit in the Cock and Bottle and talk about their exes.

The pub is open seven days a week for food and drink.

The Bird in Hand, 88 Masbro Road, Brook Green, W14 0LR
www.thebirdinhandlondon.com

In *The King of Thieves* Brian (Michael Caine) asks to meet the rest of the gang in the pub to discuss the division of the loot to ensure he and Basil (Charlie Cox) get their fair share.

They are open for food and drink every day except Monday.

Princess Victoria, 217 Uxbridge Road, W12 9DH
www.princessvictoria.co.uk

This is the headquarters of the so-called "king of the jungle" Mickey Pearson (Matthew McConaughey) in *The Gentlemen*. He appears to be assassinated in the first scene here, and then later in the film it was where Dry Eye (Henry Golding) approached him in order to buy him out of the business.

The pub was built in 1829 as a gin palace and has overnight accommodation. It is open daily for food and drink but may not serve pickled eggs.

Scarfes Bar, Rosewood Hotel, 252 High Holborn, WC1V 7EN
www.scarfesbar.com

In season three of *Killing Eve* Carolyn (Fiona Shaw) is drinking in this bar before meeting with an acquaintance and gets some important information.

The bar is open for food and drink daily.

The Apple Tree, 45 Mount Pleasant, WC1X 0AE
www.theappletreelondon.com

You can see the Apple Tree Pub in the background as Baskin (Mark Cooper Harris) drops XXX (Matthew Goode) off in *The Hatton Garden Job*.

It is seen from Phoenix Place looking back, with the white sorting office on the left.

At the time of writing the pub was temporarily closed.

**Sherlock Holmes Pub,
10 Northumberland Street, WC2N 5DB**
www.greeneking.co.uk/pubs/greater-london/sherlock-holmes

This is a Sherlock Holmes themed pub, which has a small museum with Holmes memorabilia and the upstairs restaurant is decorated to look like his sitting room.

This pub is open seven days a week for food and drink.

The Griffin, Brook Road South, Brentford, TW8 0NP
www.griffinbrentford.co.uk

In *Green Street* Pete (Charlie Hunnam) takes Matt (Elijah Wood) to The Griffin before his first football match, approaching it from Braemar Road. In the pub, Matt is introduced to Pete's football friends and learns it is the headquarters of the Green Street Elite (GSE).

The Griffin is open daily for food and drink.

Scarfes Bar, Rosewood Hotel, 252 High Holborn, WC1V 7EN

CHURCH TOUR

North

Saint Matthias Church, Wordsworth Road, N16 8DD

Season four of *Killing Eve* opens with Villanelle (Jodie Comer) in church indicating she has found religion.

This church was designed by William Butterfield in 1853. It was badly damaged in 1941 when hit by a bomb but it was restored shortly afterwards.

Hampstead Parish Church, 14 Church Row, NW3 6UU

Bill's (David Haig) funeral in *Killing Eve* was held in this church and following Frank's (Darren Boyd) terrible speech Eve (Sandra Oh) leaves in season one.

A church has been on the site since 1312 when John de Neuport is named as priest. In the eighteenth-century part of the church was still timber so money was raised to rebuild in more durable stone. Further additions and beautifications were made in the later nineteenth century.

East

St Leonard's Church, 119 Shoreditch High Street, E1 6JN

Jenny Jones (Aimee-Ffion Edwards) goes to St Leonard's Church, to meet with her mum in season two of *Luther*.

It is thought this church could be the oldest continuous Christian site in England, with the earliest record being Roman from 46 CBE. The church currently on the site was built in 1740.

George-in-the-East Crypt West, 14 Cannon Street Road, E1 0BH

Carolyn (Fiona Shaw) meets Eve in the cemetery of this church in season two of *Killing Eve*.

This church was built between 1714 and 1729 by Nicholas Hawksmoor. The original interior of the church was damaged when it was hit by a bomb in the Blitz and was replaced in the 1960s.

Christ Church Spitalfields, Commercial Street, E1 6LY

www.spitalfields.church

As Joe Goldberg (Penn Badgley) leaves the university, it is possible to see Christ Church Spitalfields in the background of the shot in season four of *You*.

Christ Church opened in 1729, as part of a drive to build fifty new churches proposed in 1711. They offer guided tours, but these must be booked in advance.

St George-in-the-East Church, Cannon Street Road, E1 0BH
In *The Long Good Friday* Harold Shand's (Bob Hoskin) mum nearly gets blown up here during the Good Friday service. The exterior shots were taken at St George-in-the-East Church.

This church was built between 1714 and 1729 by Nicholas Hawksmoor. The original interior of the church was damaged when it was hit by a bomb in the Blitz and was replaced in the 1960s.

St Patrick's Church, The Presbytery, Dundee Street, E1W 2PH
The interior shots of the Good Friday service in *The Long Good Friday* were filmed at St Patrick's Church.

St Peter's Church, St Peter's Close, Bethnal Green, E2 7AE
Jack's (Sam Spruell) body was left outside St Peter's Church in *Legend*,

George-in-the-East Crypt West, 14 Cannon Street Road, E1 0BH

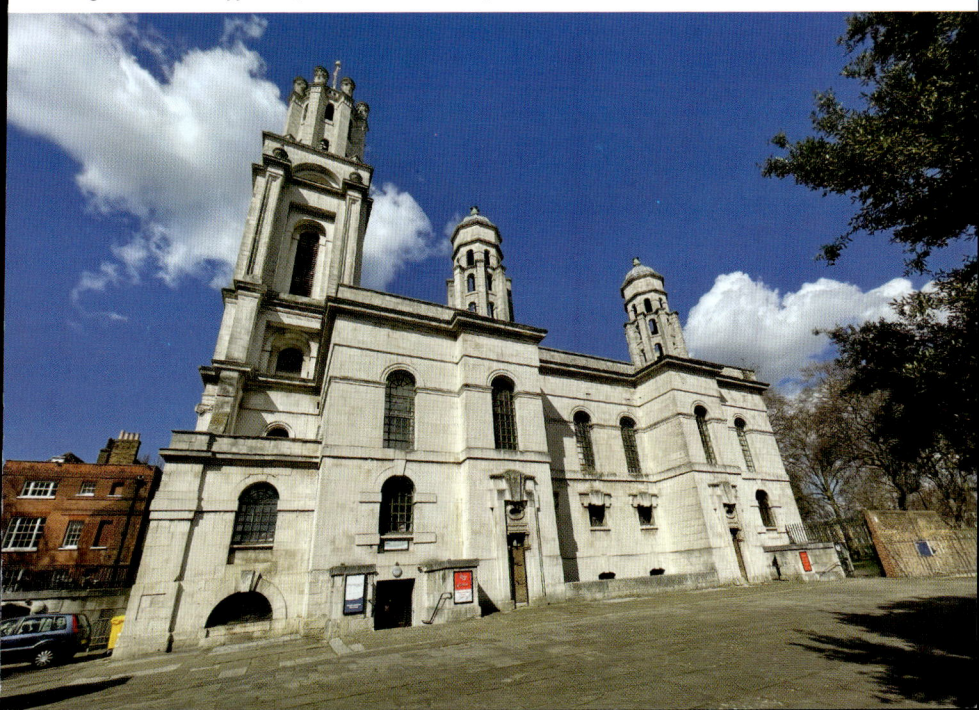

which was a stand in for the real St Mary's Church in Rotherhithe.

St Mary the Virgin Church, 1 Langley Drive, E11 2LN

In *The Hatton Garden Job* Danny (Phil Daniels) meets with Brian Reader (Larry Lamb) in the cemetery of this church to see if he is interested in taking part in the Hatton Garden job. Initially he says 'no' as he thinks he is too old.

St Anne's Church, Three Colt Street, E14 7HJ

This is where Reggie (Tom Hardy) and Frances (Emily Browning) got married in *Legend*.

This is a Nicholas Hawksmoor church consecrated in 1730 and is a Grade I listed building. The church is open to visitors Thursday - Saturday but check there are no events going on.

St Bartholemew the Great, West Smithfield, Barbican, EC1A 9DS

This church was where the memorial/funeral was held for Simon Soo (Aiden Cheng), and also where the 'Eat the Rich' protestors were standing in *You*.

St Bartholomew the Great was founded as an Augustinian priory in 1123.

Temple Church, Temple, EC4Y 7BB

The Archbishop of Canterbury (Oliver Ford Davies) in *Johnny English* is seen leaving this church. Sauvage plans to replace the archbishop for the coronation. The shot was taken at the Pump Court end of the church.

The Church of Inner and Middle Temple was consecrated in 1185 and was the Knights Templar Headquarters. The church is circular and is a replica of the Church of the Holy Sepulchre at Jerusalem. The church is occasionally opened to the public.

St Botolph-without-Bishopsgate, Bishopsgate, EC2M 3TL

In *Criminal* the Spanish anarchist, Xavier Heimdahl's (Jordi Molla) headquarters is at this church. The exterior shots were filmed here.

The current church on the site was built in 1729 and is the fourth on the site. The infant son of Elizabethan playwright, Ben Johnson is buried here.

St Lawrence Jewry C of E Church, Guildhall Yard, EC2V 5AA

The crew from *Fast and Furious 6* are involved in a car chase through London. Sniper Owen Shaw (Luke Edwards) is waiting on the top of an office block with the clock tower of this church visible behind him.

The church was initially built in 1136 and was destroyed in the Great Fire of London in 1666. Then it was rebuilt by Christopher Wren, only to be damaged in the Blitz. Like a phoenix it has once more been restored.

St Lawrence Jewry C of E Church, Guildhall Yard, EC2V 5AA (courtesy of Diego Delso, Wikimedia Commons)

St Giles' Cripplegate, Fore Street, Barbican, EC2Y 8DA

In season one of *Luther*, he meets Alice (Ruth Wilson) in St Giles' Cripplegate church to talk about his wife Zoe, and before leaving he drops his wedding ring into the collection box.

This church is one of the few surviving medieval churches in London and was built in 1090. John Milton the author of *Paradise Lost* is buried here.

West

American International Church, 79a Tottenham Court Road, W1T 4TD
www.amchurch.co.uk

In season two of *Sherlock* the sniper takes aim from the second-floor window on the stairwell of the American Church in London.

St Sophia's Greek Cathedral, Moscow Road, Bayswater, W2 4LQ
www.stsophia.org.uk

The interior shots of the St Petersburg's Church where Natalya (Izabella Scorupco) speaks with Boris (Alan Cumming) were filmed in St Sophia's Greek Cathedral.

The cathedral was built between 1877 and 1899 and designed by John Oldrid Scott. When it was built it was a church but was elevated to Cathedral in 1922. It currently has a museum telling the history of the church, although it is open by appointment only.

American International Church, 79a Tottenham Court Road, W1T 4TD

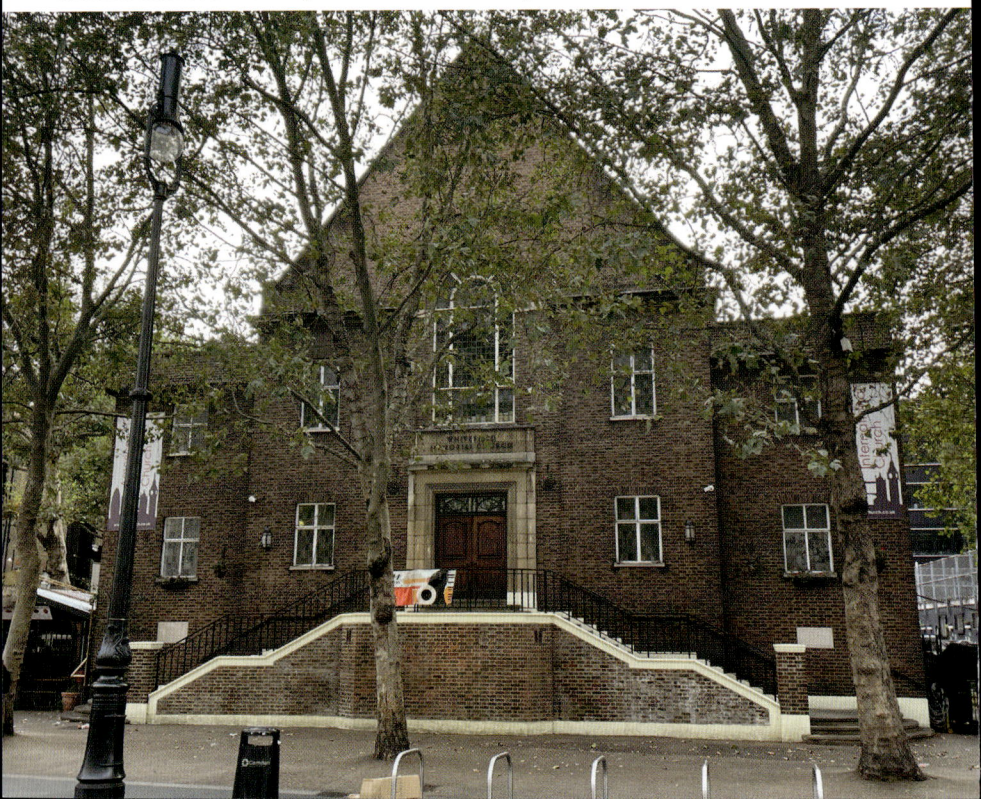

12 CEMETERY TOUR

South

Woolwich Cemetery, Camdale Road, SE18 2DS

In *The Krays* their mum Violet (Billie Whitelaw) was buried at Woolwich Cemetery. Both Krays were given leave from prison for the funeral and are seen standing by the grave with a police officer on either side of them.

Camberwell New Cemetery, SE23 3RD

In *London Boulevard* Joe (Alan Williams) is buried at Camberwell New Cemetery. The funeral is attended by Mitchel (Colin Farrell), Charlotte (Keira Knightley) and Dr Raju (Sanjeev Bhaskar).

Brompton Cemetery, Old Brompton Road, SW5 9JE

In *Golden Eye* the exterior shots of the St Petersburg Church where Natalya (Izabella Scorupco) hides, were filmed at the rear of the chapel at Brompton Cemetery – on the Fulham Road side.

It was also used in *Johnny English* as English follows the hearse here, where they disturb a funeral which was taking place.

English walks down the steps from one of chapels in the domed area near the chapel, near the Fulham Road end of the cemetery and tries to arrest the attendees of the funeral.

In *The Gentlemen* Dry Eye (Henry Golding) talks to his uncle in the car as part of his plan to take over Mickey's (Matthew McConaughey) business. This was filmed on the main thoroughfare through the centre of the cemetery with the domed chapel in the background.

West

Isleworth Cemetery, Park Road, Isleworth, TW7 6AZ

In *Calculated Risk* Steve (William Lucas) and Kip (John Rutland) lay flowers on Kip's wife's grave. She died when he was in prison. This was filmed in Isleworth Cemetery. They approach a bench which is to the right of the Pears family memorial.

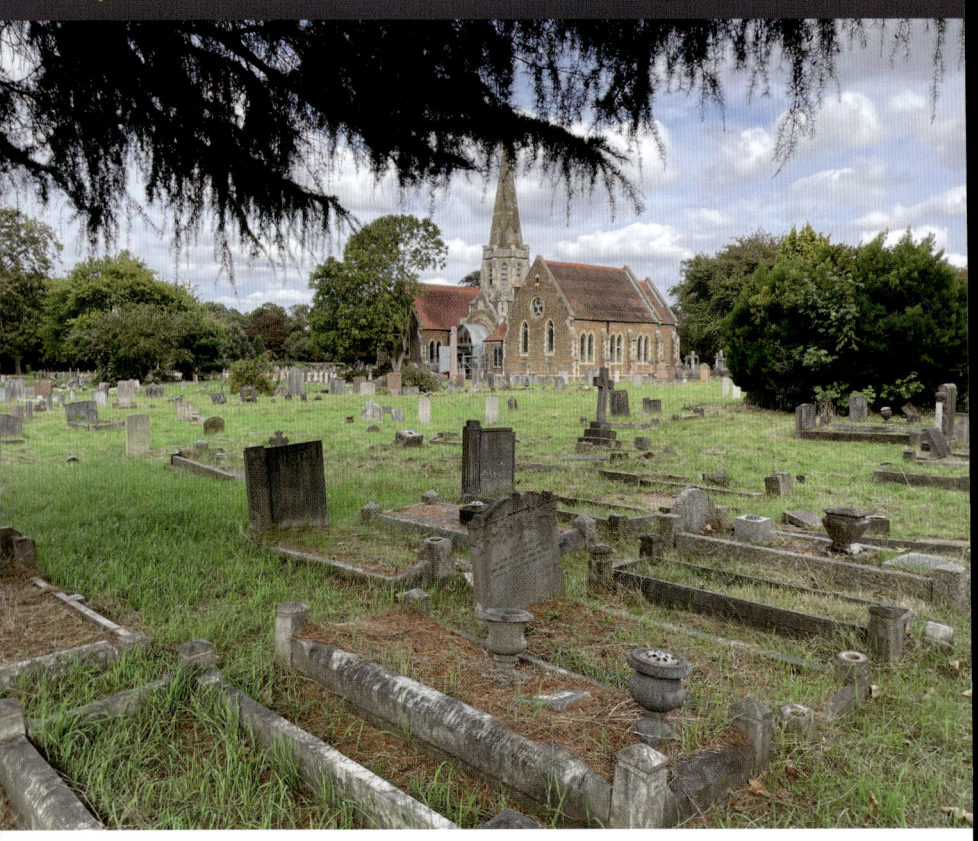

Isleworth Cemetery, Park Road, Isleworth, TW7 6AZ

PICTURE AND PLAYHOUSES TOUR

North

Carlton Cinema, 161-169 Essex Road, N1 2TS

Tony (Peter Ferdinando) and the two lads (Rob Seth-Smith and Neil Large) he met in the phone box, walk past this derelict, old cinema, in *Tony*. Today it is Gracepoint venue hire.

This used to be the Carlton Cinema, built in 1930 at the height of the Tutankhamun craze hence the Egyptian-style decoration on the facade. It is now Grade II listed but is in quite poor condition.

South

National Theatre, Upper Ground, SE1 9PX

In *Spooks: The Greater Good,* Qasim (Elyes Gabel) has a sniper covering the meeting place on Waterloo Bridge from the third-floor concrete terraces of the National Theatre and shoots Hannah Santo (Eleanor Matsuura).

Rivoli Ballroom, 350 Brockley Road, Brockley, SE4 2BY

In *Legend* the Krays' 'new' casino, Esmeralda's Barn, in Knightsbridge was filmed at the Rivoli Ballroom.

In season three of *Killing Eve,* Eve (Sandra Oh) meets Villanelle (Jodie Comer) here. Villanelle chose the venue as it was the location of the first kill she'd carried out in the UK; a high-ranking police officer who was a ballroom dancer. Eve tells Villanelle Niko (Owen McDonnell) was in hospital because Dasha (Harriet Walter) stabbed him in the neck and had blamed it on Villanelle

The Rivoli was originally built as a picture palace in 1913, and now is the only intact 1950s ballroom in London.

Royal Albert Hall, Kensington Gore, South Kensington, SW7 2AP

www.royalalberthall.com

In season three of *Killing Eve*, Carolyn (Fiona Shaw) meets Villanelle (Jodie Comer) to get answers as to who killed Mo Jafari and her son.

Royal Albert Hall, Kensington Gore, South Kensington, SW7 2AP (courtesy of Reinhold Möller, Wikimedia Commons)

The Albert Hall was originally called the Royal Albert Hall of Arts and Science, in memory of Prince Albert. It was opened in March 1871 by Queen Victoria and has held thousands of concerts, and events since then. The Hall is open for guided tours or for ticketed shows.

Empire Cinemas, 63-65 Haymarket, SW1Y 4RL
The internal shots of Café de Paris in *The Last Night in Soho*, where Eloise (Thomasin McKenzie) first sees her alter-ego Sandy (Anya Taylor-Joy) were filmed here.

This cinema has permanently closed.

New Wimbledon Theatre, 93 The Broadway, SW19 1QG
www.atgtickets.com/venues/new-wimbledon-theatre

In *The Jewel Robbery at the Grand Metropole*, the foyer was used for the scene where Poirot David Suchet) and Hastings (Hugh Fraser) go to the theatre on the opening night of

Empire Cinemas, 63-65 Haymarket, SW1Y 4RL

Pearls Before Swine. He is accosted on the stairs by a gaggle of journalists.

This Grade II listed theatre calls itself the home of London pantomime and was designed by Cecil Aubrey Massey and Roy Young and is rumoured to have included Turkish baths in the basement. It opened on Boxing Day 1910 with the pantomime, *Jack and Jill*.

East

Wilton's Music Hall, 1 Grace's Alley, Whitechapel, E1 8JB
www.wiltons.org.uk

In *Death Defying Acts* Harry Houdini (Guy Pearce) performed his act at this theatre. This was also used for the interior of 'The Regal' in *The Krays*.

Wilton's Music Hall was built in 1859 by architect Jacob Maggs and has had an interesting history. It caught fire in 1878 and had to be rebuilt. It is one of the few saloon-style music halls still in its original form and was reopened as a performance venue in 1997.

Hackney Empire, 291 Mare Street, E8 1EJ
www.hackneyempire.co.uk

The internal shots of the theatre where the big reveal was made by Poirot in *The Big Four*, were filmed inside the Hackney Empire.

The Hackney Empire was designed by architect Frank Matcham and opened in 1901 as an entertainment space starting as a music hall, with performers including Julie Andrews and Charlie Chaplin. In 1956 it was a television studio, until it was opened as a bingo hall in 1963. In the 1980s it was saved from being demolished and turned into a car park, and is now an arts centre.

West

Criterion, 224 Piccadilly, St James's, W1J 9HP
www.criterion-theatre.co.uk

In *London Boulevard* Mitchel (Colin Farrell) has dinner with Gant (Ray Winstone) in the Criterion restaurant. He turns down the deal and then leaves onto Piccadilly where he sees a large image of Charlotte on the LED display hoardings.

In *Last Night in Soho*, there was a still of Ellie's (Thomasin McKenzie) mum and grandmother in front of the Criterion Theatre.

The Criterion was opened in 1874 and is one of the few remaining independent theatres in London.

Noël Coward Theatre, 85-88 St Martin's Lane, WC2N 4AP
www.noelcowardtheatre.co.uk

In *Spooks: The Greater Good*, the suicide bomb attack on a NATO gala at the Albery Theatre kills Francis Warrender (David Harewood).

The interior was filmed in the Gaiety Theatre on the Isle of Man and the exteriors on St Martin's Lane.

The exterior was also used for the Methuselah Theatre entrance where Flossie goes for the audition which never happens in *Poirot: The Big Four*.

The theatre was first opened in 1902 and Noël Coward made his debut at the theatre in his own play *I'll Leave It to You*. It has been an active theatre since it opened.

Criterion Theatre, 218-223 Piccadilly, W1J 9HR

Richmond Theatre, 1 Little Green, Richmond, TW9 1QH

Richmond Theatre, 1 Little Green, Richmond, TW9 1QH
www.atgtickets.com/venues/richmond-theatre

The external shots of the nightclub in *The Krays*, the Regal Club, run by Ronnie (Gary Kemp) and Reggie Kray (Martin Kemp) was filmed at the Richmond Theatre.

In season four of *Killing Eve*, Hélène shows Eve the theatre her daddy had bought for her. It was also used for the exterior shots of the theatre in *Poirot: The Big Four*, where Flossie Monroe (Sarah Parish) was performing.

Designed by architect Frank Matcham the Richmond Theatre was opened in 1899. It has been an active theatre since it opened.

INDEX

Films
10 Rillington Place (1971) 70
101 Dalmatians (1996) 40
102 Dalmatians (2000) 42
11 Harrowhouse (1974) 40

A Fish Called Wanda (1988) 14

Bellman and True (1987) 44
Blue Murder at St. Trinian's (1957) 127
Buster (1988) 46, 175

Calculated Risk (1967) 46, 187
Carry On Constable (1960) 119
Clockwork Orange (1971) 119, 120
Cockneys vs Zombies (2012) 49
Criminal (2016) 112, 184

Death Defying Acts (2007) 120, 191
Die Another Day (2002) 83, 85
Dr Crippen (1962) 66
Dr No (1962) 80

Face (1997) 50
For Your Eyes Only (1981) 81
Fast and Furious 6 (2013) 76, 184

Get Lucky (2013) 52
GoldenEye (1995) 83, 86
Goldfinger (1964) 80
Green Street (2005) 120, 178, 181

Hot Fuzz (2007) 67

Jack Ryan: Shadow Recruit (2014) 78
Jason Bourne (2016) 93
Johnny English (2003) 75, 96, 178, 184, 187
Johnny English Strikes Again (2018) 100

King of Thieves (2018) 52, 180
Kingsman: The Golden Circle (2017) 101
Kingsman: The Secret Service (2014) 75, 100, 171
Kiss before dying (1991) 67

Last Night in Soho (2021) 70, 179, 190, 192
Layer Cake (2004) 122
Legend (2015) 16, 169, 172, 175, 184, 189
Lock Stock and Two Smoking Barrels (1998) 11, 12, 20, 52, 128
London Boulevard (2010) 23, 170, 171, 187, 192
Luther: The Fallen Sun (2023) 67

Men in Black International (2019) 103, 178
Mission Impossible: Rogue Nation (2015) 105
Mission: Impossible (1996) 104, 170

Octopussy (1983) 81, 83
On Her Majesty's Secret Service (1969) 80, 85

Peeping Tom (1960) 73, 178
Profile (2018) 11, 114

Quantum of Solace (2008) 88

Robbery (1967) 55, 179

Sexy Beast (2000) 58
Sherlock Holmes (2009) 123
Sherlock Holmes: A Game of Shadows (2011) 125
Skyfall (2012) 88, 90, 91
Snatch (2000) 12, 14, 28, 172
Spectre (2015) 88, 91, 93
Spooks: The Greater Good (2015) 182, 189, 192

The Bank Job (2008) 58
The Bourne Ultimatum (2007) 75
The Criminal (1999) 128

The Crying Game (1992) 115, 169, 173, 176
The Da Vinci Code (2006) 64
The Football Factory (2004) 128
The Gentlemen (2020) 29, 180, 187
The Great St. Trinian's Train
    Robbery (1966) 127
The Hatton Garden Job (2017) 31, 176,
    181, 184
The Italian Job (1969) 61
The Krays (1990) 14, 33, 169, 175, 187, 191, 193
The Living Daylights (1987) 86, 90
The Long Good Friday (1980) 36, 169, 176, 183
The World is Not Enough (1999) 83, 84
Thunderbirds (2004) 62
Tinker Tailor Soldier Spy (2011) 110
Tomorrow Never Dies (1997) 83, 87
Tony (2009) 73, 189
Trainspotting (1996) 133

V for Vendetta (2005) 116
Vendetta (2013) 69, 175, 176

TV Series
Capture - The (2019-2022) 134
Crime Traveller (1997) 135

Gold - The (2022) 138, 173

Jonathan Creek (1997-2016) 11, 135, 138, 140

Killing Eve (2018-2022) 140, 173, 180, 181, 182,
    189, 193

Luther (2010-2019) 11, 134, 150-6, 178, 182, 185

Poirot – Elephants Can Remember (2014) 157
Poirot – The Jewel Robbery At the Grand
    Metropole (1993) 156, 190
Poirot: The Big Four (2013) 158, 159, 191,
    192, 193

Sherlock (2010-2017) 160, 186

Top Boy (2011–2023) 162, 175

You (2022) 164, 170, 175, 180, 183, 184

Locations
135 Bus stop (MA), Spindrift Avenue,
    E14 9US 49

Abady House, Page Street (Grosvenor
    Estate), SW1P 4EW 46
Abingdon Street Car Park on Great College
    Street, SW1P 3RX 96, 134
Addison Road (68), W14 8JL 23
Agatha Christie Memorial, Cranbourn Street,
    WC2H 7AB 167
Air Street (5), W1J 0AD 105
Albert Hall Mansions, 31-48 Kensington Gore,
    SW7 2AW 147
Aldersgate Street (97), EC1A 4JP 150
Aldwych Station, Surrey Street, WC2R 2ND 7,
    33, 46, 59, 69, 76, 78, 118, 162
Alexandra and Ainsworth Estate, Rowley Way,
    Camden, NW8 0SN 100, 103, 135
Alwyne Road (6), N1 2HH 117
American International Church, 79a Tottenham
    Court Road, W1T 4TD 10, 162, 186
Anchor Tavern, 34 Park Street, SE1 9EF 104, 170
Annabel's, 46 Berkeley Square, Mayfair, W1J
    5AT 30, 40
Ark Walworth Academy Shorncliffe Road, SE1
    5UJ 163
Armourers Hall, 81 Coleman Street,
    EC2R 5BI 147
Arnold Circus, Calvert Avenue, Bethnal
    Green, E2 7JP 155
Athenaeum Club, 107 Pall Mall, St. James's,
    SW1Y 5ER 108, 122
Aubrey House, 7 Maida Avenue, W2 1TQ 14
Austin Friars, EC2N 2HG 107
Australia House, Strand WC2B 4LA 125
Averard Hotel, 16 Lancaster Gate, W2 3LH 9,
    147, 148

Babington House, Redcross Way, SE1 1EZ 108
Baker Street (189), NW1 6UY 58
Bancroft Road (370), Bethnal Green, E1 4BU 51
Bank of England, Threadneedle Street, EC3V 3LA 53
Bank Underground Station, Royal Exchange, EC3V 3LR 112, 121
Banking Hall, 14 Cornhill, EC3V 3ND 145
Barbican Centre (Plaza) Silk Street, Barbican, EC2Y 8DS 143
Barbican Centre, Upper Frobisher Crescent, Silk Street, EC2Y 8HD 8, 88, 89
Barbican Launderette, 2 Fann Street, Barbican, EC2Y 8AF 148
Barclay's Bank, Goldsmiths' Hall, Foster Lane, EC2V 6BN 59
Bartholomew Lane (41), EC2N 2AX 100
Bartholomew Street (27), SE1 4AL 11, 25, 26
Bateman's Row (24), EC2A 3HH 154
Battersea Bridge, Battersea Bridge Road, SW10 0DQ 23
Battersea Park, SW11 4NJ 42
Battersea Power Station, 188 Kirtling Street, Nine Elms, SW8 5BN 78, 161
BBC Broadcasting House, Langham Street, Langham Street, W1B 3DF 135
Bell Yard, WC2A 2JR 107
Belvedere Road (3A/B), SE1 7GP *8, 98, 99*
Bernelių Uzeiga, Shepherd's Inn, 485 High Road, Leytonstone E11 4PG 31
Berry Brothers and Rudd, 3 St. James's Street, SW1A 1EF 103
Bethnal Green Town Hall, Cambridge Heath Road, E2 9NF 21, 128
Big Ben, 67 Bridge Street, SW1A 2PW 164
Big Moe's Diner, 3 Jenkins Lane, IG11 0AD 69
Billy's Café, 4 Pritchard's Road, Bethnal Green, E2 9AP 51
Birkbeck Tavern, 45 Langthorne Road, E11 4HL 69, 176

Birstall Road, N15 5EN 128
Black Prince, 6 Black Prince Road, Kennington, SE11 6HS 100, 171
Blackfriars Crown Court, 1-15 Pocock Street, SE1 0BT 163
Blackfriars Road, SE1 9UD 150
Blackman's Shoes, Cheshire Street, Shoreditch, E2 6EH 7, 21
Blackwall Tunnel, SE10 0QE 52
Blake Tower, 2 Fann Street, EC2Y 8AF 155
Blomfield Road (31), W9 1AA 40
Blythe House, 23 Blythe Road, West Kensington, W14 0QX 110
Borough Market, SE1 9AL 8, *113*, 114
Boscobel Place, SW1W 9PE 161
Bottle Kiln, Walmer Road, W11 4NN 57
Botts Mews, W2 5AG 7, 23, *24*
Brace Orthodontist, 15 Artillery Passage, E1 7LJ 67
Brent Cross Shopping Centre, Prince Charles Drive, NW4 3FP 88
Brick Lane (124-126), E1 6RU 116
Brick Lane (63A), E1 6QL 67
Bridgeman Road, N1 1BN 118
Broadgate Tower, 201 Bishopsgate, EC2M 3AB 90
Brompton Cemetery, Old Brompton Road, SW5 9JE 30, 87, 96, 105, 124, 187
Brunswick Gardens (40), Kensington, W8 4AL 42
Buckingham Gate (62), SW1E 6AJ 135
Buckingham Palace, SW1A 1AA 8, 85, 99
Building 3 North London Business Park, Oakleigh Road South, N11 1GN 78
Burlington Arcade, 51 Piccadilly, W1J 0QJ 7, 41, 42, 156

Cadogan Square (101), SW1X 0DY 121
Cadogan Square (82), SW1X 0EA 90
Café de Paris, 3-4 Coventry Street, W1D 6BL 7, 18, 35

Café Laville, 453 Edgware Road, W2 1TH 135
Café Lazeeze, 88 St John Street,
    Farringdon, EC1M 4EH 128
Camberwell Grove (64), SE5 8RF 150
Camberwell New Cemetery, SE23 3RD 24, 187
Camelford House, 89 Albert
    Embankment, SE1 7TP 91
Campden Street (47-8), W8 7ET 167
Canada Square (1), E14 5DY 96
Canary Wharf Station, E14 5LL 103
Cannon Place, 78 Cannon Street, EC4N 6HN 76
Canrobert Street (79), E2 6PX 61
Caradoc Street (32), SE10 9AG 16, 33
Carlton Cinema, 161-169 Essex Road, N1 2TS
    73, 74, 189
Carlton House Terrace (10), St. James's, SW1Y
    5ED 161
Carnaby Street, W1F 9PS 72
Castle Baynard Tunnel, Castle Baynard
    Street, EC4V 4EA 91
Cat and Mutton Pub, 76 Broadway Market, E8
    4RA 46, 175
Catherine Place (15), SW1E 6DX 39
Cavita, 56-60 Wigmore Street, W1U 2RZ 7, 37
Cedra Court, Cazenove Road, N16 6AT 18
Central St Giles, WC2H 8AB 134
Chalk Farm footbridge, Regent's Park Road,
    NW1 8JA 118
Chapel, Old Royal Naval College, SE10 9NN
    103
Charing Cross Underground, Strand, WC2N
    5HF 75, 142
Charles Hocking House, 118 Bollo Bridge
    Road, W3 8SJ 150,
Charles Street (16), W1J 5DS 46
Charterhouse Mews, EC1M 6AH 9, *157*, 158
Chesham Street (37), SW1X 8NQ 116
Cheshire Street (72), E2 6EH 52
Chicken Run, 42 Toynbee Street, E1 7NE 114
Chimney Memorial, 23 Wesley Avenue, E16
    1UR 112
Chiswick Town Hall, Heathfield Terrace, W4
    4JN 140
Christ Church Spitalfields, Commercial
    Street, E1 6LY 164, 182,
Church Road (187), NW10 9EE 140
Church Street (8), E15 3HX 121
Cinema Museum, The Master's House,
    2 Dugard Way (off Renfrew Road),
    SE11 4TH 167
City View Hotel, 11 Church Street, E15 3HU 121
Citypoint, 1 Ropemaker Street, Barbican,
    EC2V 9HT 139
Clapton Hart Pub, 231 Lower Clapton Road,
    E5 8EG 142, 175
Clapton Vax Centre, 103 Lower Clapton Road,
    Lower Clapton, E5 0NP 154
Clarissa Street (27), E8 4HJ 73
Clayton Hotel, Chiswick High Road, W4
    5RY 140
Clerkenwell Green, EC1R 0DU 15
Clock House, Rutland Mews West - SW7 1NZ 58
Cloth Fair, Smithfield, EC1A 7JQ 116
Cock and Bottle, 17 Needham Road, W11 2RP
    148, 180
College of Arms, 130 Queen Victoria
    Street EC4V 4BT 9, 80, 124, *125*
Connaught Bridge, Silvertown, E16 2BU 114
Corbett's Lane, SE16 2BE 121
Corbiere House, Balmes Road, N1 5SR 30
Corbridge Crescent, Cambridge Heath, E2
    9EZ 101
Cornwall Gardens (69), SW7 4BA 164
Coronet Street, between Hoxton
    Square and Boot Street, N1 6HD 18, 116
County Hall Building, Belvedere Road, SE1
    7PB 104
Courthouse Hotel Shoreditch, 337 Old
    Street, EC1V 9LL 154, 155
Covent Garden, Bedford Street, WC2E 9ED 139
Criterion Theatre, 218-223 Piccadilly, St.
    James's, W1J 9HR 10, 25, 70, 192

Cromwell Road (147), SW5 0TH 143
Crossness Pumping Station, Abbey Wood, SE2 9AQ 123
Crown Close (3-5), Bow, E3 2JH 51
Crowne Plaza London Shoreditch, 100 Shoreditch High Street, E1 6JQ 151
Crutched Friars (3), EC3N 2HT 110
Crystal Palace Park, Thicket Road, SE19 2BA 62
Cubitt Town Library, 52 Strattondale Street, E14 3HG 50
Curzon Bloomsbury, The Brunswick Centre, WC1N 1AW 9, 136, *137*

Dagmar Court, Manchester Road, Isle of Dogs, E14 3JF 51
Darkhorse, 16 Victory Parade, East Village, E20 1FS 163
Dean Rees House, Queen Mary University of London, Charterhouse Square, EC1M 6BQ 157
Delamare Terrace, W2 6PF 56
Denbigh Close (18), W11 2QH 8, 61
Doyles Tavern, 359 Pentonville Road, N7 9DQ 23, 170
Drapers' Hall, Throgmorton Street, EC2N 2DQ 87
Duke of York Column and Steps, SW1Y 5AJ 42
Dulwich Village (9), SE21 7BU 26

East Finchley Underground Station, High Road, N2 0NW 120
Eaton Place (100), SW1X 8LW 116
Eaton Square (44), SW1W 9BD 161
Elegance Jewellers, 8-9 Greville Street, EC1N 8SB 53
Elm Court, Middle Temple, EC4Y 7AH 8, 107
Ely Court, Hatton Garden, EC1N 6RY 7, 53
Emirates Stadium, Arsenal Football Club, 75 Hornsey Road, N7 7AJ 30
Empire Cinemas, 63-65 Haymarket, SW1Y 4RL 10, 70, 190

Endsleigh Gardens (8) WC1H 0EG 7, 59
Excel London, Royal Victoria Dock, 1 Western Gateway, E16 1XL 134
Exchange House, Primrose Street, Broadgate, EC2A 2EG 79

Fabric Nightclub, 77A Charterhouse Street, EC1M 6HJ 9, 140, 165
Fantasia Grill House, 28 Praed Street, W2 1NH 8, 94, *95*
Farringdon Tube Station, Cowcross Street, EC1M 6BY 8, 117
Fen Shang Princess, Southern Star Cumberland Basin, Prince Albert Road, NW1 7SS 30
Fen Street, E16 1JS 49
Fenchurch Street Station, Fenchurch Place, EC3M 4AJ 121
Fenchurch Street, EC3M 5JE 110
Feng Shui Inn, 6 Gerrard Street, W1D 5PG 160
Finchley Nurseries, Burtonhole Lane, NW7 1AS 67
First National Bank of Chicago, First Chicago House, 90 Long Acre, WC2E 9RA 67
Fishmonger's Hall Wharf, Thames Path, EC4R 3AE 54
Fleece House, 160 Abbey Street, SE1 3NR 34
Florence Nightingale Statue, St James, SW1Y 4AR 102
Florin Court, 6-9 Charterhouse Square, Barbican, EC1M 6EU 9, 157, 159
Floris, 89 Jermyn Street, St James's, SW1Y 6JH 147
Formosa Street (44), W9 2JS 122
Four Seasons Hotel London, 10 Trinity Square, EC3N 4AJ 90, 145, 164
Fournier Street (3), E1 6QE 115
Freemasons' Hall, 60 Great Queen Street, WC2B 5AZ 96, 124

Gatehouse Block, Gibson Gardens, N16 7HL 17
Gee Street, EC1V 163

George Eliot Primary School, Marlborough Hill, London NW8 0NH 56
George-in-the-East Crypt West, 14 Cannon Street Road, E1 0BH 9, 36, 142, *182*, 183
Gilbert Scott Restaurant, St Pancras Renaissance Hotel, Euston Road, NW1 2AR 146
Giltspur Street, EC1A 7AA 116
Glengall Bridge, Millwall Inner Dock, Isle of Dogs, E14 9QY 84
Globe Tavern, 8 Bedale Street, Borough Market, SE1 9AL 9, 166, 170
Gloucester Mews, W2 3HE 133
Gloucester Road Underground Ltd, Gloucester Road, South Kensington, SW7 4SF 164
Gloucester Terrace (207), W2 6HX 64
Godfrey Phillips, 112 Jerome Street, E1 6BX 154
Golden Jubilee Bridge, WC2N 6NU 62
Goldsmiths' Hall, Foster Lane, EC2V 6BN 59, 61, 142
Goodge Place (8), W1T 4SG 72
Grand Avenue, Smithfield Market, EC1A 9PS 7, 45, 46, 99, 154
Great George Street, SW1P 3AA 91, 103, 127
Great Windmill Street, W1D 7LA 105
Greek Street (13), W1D 4DN 72
Green Dragon Court, Borough, SE1 9AW 128
Greenfield Road, E1 147
Greenland Dock, Swedish Quay, SE16 7UF 9, 151
Greenland Surrey Quays Pier, SE16 7TY 95
Grosvenor Gardens, SW1W 0RP 56
Grosvenor Square (24), W1A 1AE 112
Guy's Hospital, SE1 9GU 9, 140, *141*

Hackney Empire, 291 Mare Street, E8 1EJ 159, 191
Hackney Free Parochial School, 39 Wilton Way, E8 3ED 34
Haggerston Park, Yorkton Street, E2 8NH 154

Hamley's Toy Store, 188-196 Regent Street, W1B 5BT 147
Hammersmith Apollo, 45 Queen Caroline Street, W6 9QH 103
Hampstead 1 Pond, Hampstead Heath, NW5 1QR 110
Hampstead High Street Police Station, 26 Rosslyn Hill, NW3 1PA 7, 43
Hampstead Parish Church, 14 Church Row, NW3 6UU 140, 182
Hanover Arms, 326 Kennington Park Road, SE11 4PP 23, 171
Hanwell Library, Cherington Road, Hanwell, W7 3HL 119
Harbour Square Park, Timber Quay Park, 22 Lovegrove Walk, E14 9PZ 50
Hare Row, Cambridge Heath, E2 9BY 76
Harwood Arms, Walham Grove, SW6 1QJ 128, 173
Hat & Mitre Court, EC1M 4EF 7, 32, *33*
Hatton Garden (19-21), EC1N 8BA 55
Hatton Garden (24), EC1N 8BQ 53
Hatton Garden (37-38), EC1N 8EB 7, 14
Hatton Garden (78-83), EC1N 8JS 75
Hatton Garden (88-90), EC1N 8PN 7, 31, *32*, 53
Hendon Police Training College, Aerodrome Road, NW9 5JE 67
Heron Square, Richmond TW9 1EH 138
High Street (467), Leytonstone, E11 4JU 33
Highbury Hill (11), Islington, N5 1SU 20
Hijingo Bingo, 90 Worship Street, EC2A 2BA
Hillfield Park (25), Muswell Hill, N10 3QT 155
HMP Pentonville, Caledonian Road, N7 8TT 23
HMP Wormwood Scrubs 160 Du Cane Road, W12 0AN 8, 61, 66, 150
Holborn Police Station, 15 Lamb's Conduit Street, WC1N 3NR 8, 101
Holland Park Avenue (98) W11 3RB 7, 24
Hornsey Town Hall, The Broadway, N8 9JJ 142
Horse Guards Avenue, SW1A 2HU 83, 93
Houses of Parliament, Bridge Street, SW1A 2PW 118

Hoxton Square (8-9), N1 6NU 116, 169
HQTS Lord Amory, 631 Manchester Road, Docklands E14 3NU 52
Huntingdon Street (1), London Royal Docks, E16 1HS 50
Huntsman, 11 Savile Row, W1S 3PG 100, 101
Hyde Park Bandstand, W2 2UH 42

Imperial College, Prince Consort Road, South Kensington SW7 2BH 101
Inglis Barracks, Mill Hill, NW7 1FE 111
Institute of Director's Club, 116 Pall Mall, St James's, SW1Y 5ED 128
Isleworth Cemetery, Park Road, Isleworth TW7 6AZ 10, 47, 187, *188*
Italian Bear Chocolate, 29 Rathbourne Place, W1T 1JG 73

James Hammett House, Diss Street, Dorset Estate, E2 7QX 18
James Smith & Sons, Hazelwood House, 53 New Oxford Street, WC1A 1BL 8, 108, *109*
Jamie's Ludgate Hill, 47 Ludgate Hill, EC4M 7JZ 104
Jamme Masjid, Brick Lane, E1 6QL 114
Jermyn Street, SW1Y 6ST 42
John Adam Street (8), WC2N 6EZ 96
Jolly Gardeners, 49-51 Black Prince Road, SE11 6AB 28, 172
Jubilee Gardens, Belvedere Road, SE1 7PG 8, 62
JW Marriott Grosvenor House Hotel, Park Lane, W1K 7TN 58

Kensal Green Cemetery, Harrow Road, W10 4RA 158
Kensington High Street (99), (Kensington Roof Gardens) W8 5SA 39
Kent Court, 14 Kent Street, E2 8NU 154
Kiki's Nail Salon, Freemasons Road, E16 163
King Charles Street Arch, 100 Parliament Street, SW1A 2NH 100
King George V Dock, E16 2LH 39
King's Head, Poplar Place, Bayswater, W2 4AH 30
Kynance Mews (10), SW7 4QP 164

Ladywell Leisure Centre, 261 Lewisham High Street, SE13 6AY 37
Lamb & Flag, 24 James Street, W1U 1EL 152, 178
Lambeth Bridge, Lambeth Road, SE1 7LB 76, 100, 108
Lancresse Court, De Beauvoir Town, N1 5TG 30
Landmark London, 222 Marylebone Road, NW1 6JQ 136
Lansdowne Gardens (28), SW8 2EG 151
Leadenhall Market, Gracechurch Street, EC3V 1LT 8, 96, *97*, 122, 178
Leader's Gardens, Putney Embankment, SW15 1LW 57
Lee Navigation Canal, Three Mill Lane, E3 3DU 105
Leicester Square, WC2H 7AL 40
Leinster Gardens (23-24), W2 3AN 162
Leinster Square (43), W2 4PU 45
Lemonia, 89 Regent's Park Road, NW1 8UY 139
Les Ambassadeurs Club, 5 Hamilton Place, W1J 7ED 80
Leven Road, Poplar, E14 0NB 50
Leyton Orient, Brisbane Road, E10 5NF 57
Lilian Knowles House, Sanctuary Students, 47-50 Crispin Street, E1 6HQ 8, 115
Lime Street (40), EC3M 7AW 122
Lincoln's Inn, 11 New Square, WC2A 3QB 164
Lindsey Street, Barbican, EC1A 9EJ 96
Liverpool Street Underground Station, Liverpool Street, EC2M 1QT 7, 51, 104, 145, 151,
Lloyd Square (18), Islington, WC1X 9AJ 8, 111
Lloyds Bank, 185 Baker Street, NW1 6XB 58
Lloyds Bank, Wax Chandlers Hall, Wax Chandlers Hall, 6 Gresham Street, EC2V 7AD 61

Lock & Co, 6 St James's Street, SW1A 1EF 101
London Aquatics Centre, E20 2ZQ 147
London City Airport, Hartmann Road, E16 2PB 54, 114
London School of Economics, Houghton Street, WC2A 2AE 78
London Wall (140), Barbican, EC2Y 5DN 134
Lothbury, EC2R 7HH 100
Lucky Voice Karaoke Bar, 84 Chancery Lane, WC2A 1DL 150
Lund Point, E15 2JN 155

Maitland Chambers, 7 Stone Buildings, WC2A 3S2 158
Malaysia House, 57 Trafalgar Square, WC2N 5DU 8, 83
Maple Street, Fitzrovia, W1T 4BN 72
Marble Arch, W2 2UH 8, 102
Marylebone Station, Melcombe Place, NW1 6JJ 57, 156
Mattison Road (63-65), N4 1BG 52
Maughan Library, Chancery Lane, WC2A 1LR 96
May Gardens (15), Wembley, HA0 1DU 54
Melbury Road (8), W14 8LR 73
Mentmore Terrace (11), E8 3PN 114
Middle Pond, Hampstead Heath, NW5 1QR 46
Middle Temple Lane, EC4Y 9AA 123
Midlands Bank, Goldsmiths' Hall Gresham Street, EC2V 7HN 61
Millennium Dome/O2 Arena, Peninsula Square, SE10 0DX 84
Millennium Mills, West Silvertown 1, 23 Rayleigh Road, E16 1UR 154
Millwall Football Ground, Senegal Road, SE16 3LP 9, 129, *130*
Millwall Inner Dock, E14 9RD 52, 84
Milson Road (37), Hammersmith, W14 0LD 54
Ministry of Defence, Whitehall Court, SW1A 2HB 81
Minster Court, Mincing Lane, EC3R 7BD 40

Moorfields (44), EC2Y 9AL 155
Moorfields, EC2Y 9AL
Moorgate (5-6), EC2M 6XB
Moreland Street (39), Clerkenwell, EC1V 8BB
Mountford Place and Kennington Road, SE11 4DB 23
Mount Pleasant (371), WC1X 0BD 104

National Gallery, Trafalgar Square, WC2N 5DN (Room 34) 90
National Liberal Club, 1 Whitehall Place, SW1A 2HE 138
National Theatre, Upper Ground, SE1 9PX 8, 110, 189
Neo Bankside, 72 Holland Street, SE1 9NX 31
New Billingsgate Fish Market, Trafalgar Way, E14 5ST
New Concordia Wharf, 3 Mill Street, SE1 2BG
New Moon Pub, Leadenhall Market, Gracechurch Street, EC3V 1LT
New Scotland Yard, Victoria Embankment, SW1A 2JL 9, 160, *161*
New Square, Lincoln's Inn, WC2A 3RJ 9, 16, 78, 159, 164
New Wimbledon Theatre, 93 The Broadway, SW19 1QG 156, 190
Newman Arms, 23 Rathbone Street, W1 1NG 73, 178
Nobel House, Millbank, SW1P 3HX 108
Noël Coward Theatre, 85-88 St Martin's Lane, WC2N 4AP 110, 159, 192
North Gower Street (187), NW1 2NJ 160
North Street, Isleworth TW7 6RE 7, 48
Northcote Arms, 110 Grove Green Road, E11 4EL 69, 175
Northcote Road, Battersea, SW11 1NP 139
Northumberland Avenue (corner of Great Scotland Yard), SW1A 2BD 55
Northumberland House, Lower Square, Isleworth TW7 6RL 7, 47, *48*
Number One Café, 36-38 Well Street, E9 7PX 163

Oakdene (4), Ealing W13 8AW 54
Old Bailey, EC4M 7EH 8, 66, 67, *68*, 116, 160
Old Billingsgate, 1 Old Billingsgate Walk (Riverside), 16 Lower Thames Street, EC3R 6DX 165
Old Billingsgate, 1 Old Billingsgate Walk, EC3R 6DX 76
Old Compton Street, Soho, W1D 5NG 72
Old English Garden, Victoria Park, Grove Road, E3 5TB 163
Old Royal Naval College, King William Walk, Greenwich SE10 9NN 9, 18, 81,103, 124, 125, *126*
Old War Office Building, Horse Guards Avenue, SW1A 2EU 83
Oldfield Grove Road (122), SE16 2NE 9, 131
Onslow Gardens (69), South Kensington, SW7 3QD 15
Ornamental Canal, Wapping Lane, Tobacco Dock, E1W 2JX 84
Orsman Road (15), N1 5RA 28
Oval Tube Station, Corner of Clapham Road and Harleyford Road, SE11 4PP 23
Oxford Street (376-384), W1C 1JY 56
Oxo Tower Foreshore, SE1 9PH 160

Paddington Basin, North Wharf Road, W2 1LF 93
Paddington Platform One, Paddington Station, Praed Street, W2 1HB 7, 60, *61*
Paddington Station, Praed Street, W2 1HB 7, 36, 37, 44, 121, 123
Palace Court (15), W2 4LP 9, 127
Palace Gardens Terrace (46/48), W8 4PX 40
Parish Church Of St Luke, Sydney Street, SW3 6NH 42
Park Street, Borough, SE1 9AB 7, 21, 42, 104, 170
Peacock Gym, 8-9 Caxton Street North, E16 1JL 69
Pedley Street, Shoreditch, E1 5FQ 20, 52

Pellicci's Café, 332 Bethnal Green Road, E2 0AG 17
Peninsula Heights, 93 Albert Embankment, SE1 7TY 62
Percy Passage, Fitzrovia, W1T 1RH 72
Petticoat Lane Market, Wentworth Street, E1 7TB 154
Piccadilly (150), St James's, W1J 9BR 164
Piccadilly Circus Underground Station, W1B 5DQ 105
Piccadilly Circus, SW1Y 4QF 9, 67, 105, 117, 129
Porchester Centre, Queensway, W2 5HS 54
Pottery Lane (18), W11 4LZ 7, 24
Premier House, 12-13 Hatton Garden, EC1N 8AN 28
Primrose Hill, NW3 3DS 139
Princelet Street (4), E1 6QH 154
Princess Victoria, 217 Uxbridge Road, W12 9DH 29, 180
Printworks, Surrey Quays Road, SE16 7PJ 135
Priory Church of St Bartholomew the Great, Cloth Fair, Barbican, EC1A 7JQ 124
Prospect of Whitby, 57 Wapping Wall, E1W 3SH 164, 175
Providence Square Lookout, 49 Bermondsey Wall W, SE1 2AX 138
Putney Bridge, SW6 3JL 70

Queen Alexandra's House, Bremner Road, Kensington Gore, South Kensington, SW7 2QT 17, 67, 111
Queen Mary and Westfield's College, 327 Mile End Road, Bethnal Green, E1 4NS 128
Queen Victoria Street (53), EC4N 4SG 55
Queen's Elm, 241 Fulham Road, SW3 6HY 129
Queen's Gate Mews, Kensington, SW7 5QJ 58, 122
Queensway (117), W2 4SJ 45

RAF Northolt, West End Road, Ruislip, HA4 6NG 80, 81, 84
Rawstorne Street, Finsbury, EC1V 7AJ 116

Redchurch Street (85), E2 7DJ 139
Reels Amusements, 127 Broadway, West Ealing, W13 9BE 28
Regency Cafe, 17-19 Regency Street, SW1P 4BY 122
Regent Square Gardens, WC1H 8HZ 8, 73, 74
Regents Street, SW1Y 4PE 164
Renaissance London Heathrow Hotel, Bath Road, Hounslow, TW6 2AQ 153
Repton Boxing Club, 116 Cheshire Street, E2 6EG 7, 21, 29
Richmond Theatre, 1 Little Green, Richmond TW9 1QJ 10, 34, 138, 148, 158, 193
RiDa East, 10a Blossom Street E1 6PL 58
Ridley Road Market, St. Mark's Rise, E8 2PD 163
Ridley Road, E8 2NR 73
River Café, 14 Station Road Approach, SW6 3UH 54
Riverside Walk, Eye Pier, SE1 7PB 62
Rivoli Ballroom, 350 Brockley Road, SE4 2BY 17, 145, 156, 189
Robert's Place, Clerkenwell, EC1R 0BB 15
Rosie O'Grady's, 204 Manor Place, SE17 3BN 29
Rotherhithe Tunnel, 157 Rotherhithe Street, SE16 5QJ6 9, 121
Roundwood Park, Willesden Green, NW10 3SH 139
Royal Albert Hall, Kensington Gore, South Kensington, SW7 2AP 10, 146, 189, *190*
Royal Eagle Hotel, 26-30 Craven Road, W2 3QP 133
Royal Exchange (9), EC3V 3LL 112
Royal Lancaster Hotel, Lancaster Terrace, W2 2TY 61
Royal Oak Pub, 73 Columbia Road, E2 7RG 20, 34, 175
Royal Observatory, Blackheath Avenue, SE10 8XJ 123
Royal Victoria Dock Bridge, 1 Western Gateway, E16 1XL 69
Royal Victoria Dock, Canning Town, E16 3BT 84
Royal Victoria Dock, Footbridge, Gallions Point Marina, E16 1XL 166
Rules Restaurant, 34-35 Maiden Lane, Covent Garden, WC2E 7LB 8, 91, *92*
Russell Square Gardens, WC1H 0XG 9, 143, *144*, 160

Sackville Street (7), W1S 3DE 58
Saint Matthias Church, Wordsworth Road, N16 8DD 147, 182
Samuda Estate, Manchester Road, E14 3HA 162
Sandringham Road, Dalston, E8 2LL 50
Sarum Chase, 23 West Heath Road, Hampstead NW3 7UU 7, 42, *43*
Savile Club, 69 Brook Street, W1K 4ER 147
Savile Row (11), W1S 3PG 100, 101
Savoy Steps (behind the Coal Hole Pub, Aldwych), WC2R 0EX 128
Savoy, The Strand, WC2R 0EZ 7, *38*, 39
Scarfes Bar, Rosewood Hotel, 252 High Holborn, WC1V 7EN 9, 145, 181
Schiller International University, 51-55 Waterloo Road, SE1 8TX 125
Sclater Street (29), E1 6HT 134
Sclater Street (90-98), E1 6HR 155
Seething Lane Garden, Seething Lane, EC3N 4AT 166
Senate House University of London, Malet Street, WC1E 7HU 8, 76, *77*, 79
Serpentine Bar and Kitchen, Hyde Park, Serpentine Road, W2 2UH 56, 102, 179
Serpentine Bridge, Hyde Park, W2 2UH 146
Sessions Art Club, Knotel, 24 Clerkenwell Green, EC1R 0NA 148
Seven Sisters Tube Station, Seven Sisters Road Tottenham, N15 5LA 128
Seymour Leisure Centre, Seymour Place, W1H 5TJ 147
Sheffield Terrace (58), Holland Park, W8 7NA 167
Shepherd's Bush Market, W12 8DF 48

Sheraton Grand London, Park Lane, 51-53 Brick Street, W1J 7DH 157
Sherlock Holmes Museum, 221b Baker Street, NW1 6XE 9, 168
Sherlock Holmes Pub, 10 Northumberland Street, WC2N 5DB 167, 181
Sherlock Holmes Statue, Baker Street Underground Station Marylebone Road, NW1 5LJ 9, 168
Shoreditch Balls, 333 Old Street, EC1V 9LE 115, 176
Silwood Street (55), SE16 2AW 9, 133
Sinclair House, 6 Hastings Street, WC1H 9PZ 136
Sirinham Point, 4 Meadow Road, SW8 1QB 24
Smallbrook Mews, Bayswater, W2 3BN 133
SOAS University of London Library, Russell Square, WC1H 0XG 114
Soho Square, Soho, W1D 3QP 72
Somerset House, Strand, WC2R 1LA 8, 86, 87
Somerset Square (29), W14 8EF 23
Sonic Digital, 71 Praed Street, Tyburnia, W2 1NS 8, 93
Sotheby's, 34-35 New Bond Street, W1A 2RP 8, *82*, 83
South Bank Skate Park, 337-338 Belvedere Road, SE1 8XT 161
South Haringey School, 110 Pemberton Road, Haringey Ladder, N4 1BA 52
Southwark Bridge, EC4V 3BG 151
Southwood Lawn Road (32), Highgate, N6 5SH 50
Spencer Street, EC1V 0HB 50
Spit and Sawdust, 21 Bartholomew Street, SE1 4AL 7, 25, 26, 27, 170
Spring Bridge Road (4), Ealing, W5 2AA 31
Spring Gardens (7), SW1 2BU 8, *92*, 93
St Albans Terrace, W6 8HJ 129
St Anne's Church, Three Colt Street, E14 7HJ 18, 184
St Bartholemew The Great, West Smithfield, Barbican, EC1A 9DS 165, 184
St Bartholomew's Hospital, W Smithfield, EC1A 7BE 165, 184
St Botolph-without-Bishopsgate, Bishopsgate, EC2M 3TL 114, 184
St Cross Street (14), EC1N 8UN 32
St George-In-The-East Church, Cannon Street Road, E1 0BH 36, 183
St Giles Cripplegate Fore Street, Barbican, EC2Y 8DA 152, 185
St James's Park, SW1A 2BJ 42
St John Street, EC1 4AZ 7, 8, 20, 105, 128
St John's Gate, 26 St John's Lane, EC1M 4BU 7, 15
St John's Square (53-54), EC1V 4JL 79
St Katharine's Dock, 50 St Katharine's Way, E1W 1LA 39
St Lawrence Jewry C of E Church, Guildhall Yard, EC2V 5AA 9, 76, 184, *185*
St Leonard's Church, 119 Shoreditch High Street, E1 6JN 155, 182
St Magnus House Passageway, 3 Lower Thames Street, EC3R 6HD 134
St Martin's Lane Hotel, 45 St Martin's Lane, WC2N 4HX 8, 122, *123*
St Mary the Virgin Church, 1 Langley Drive, E11 2LN 31, 184
St Mary's Church, Church Road, Hanwell, W7 3BZ 119
St Mary's Mansions, St Pancras Euston Road, N1C 4QP 135, 138
St Pancras Renaissance Hotel, Euston Road, NW1 2AR 108, 146
St Pancras Station, Euston Road, N1C 4QP 44, 87, 147
St Patrick's Church, The Presbytery, Dundee Street, E1W 2PH 37, 183
St Peter's Church, St. Peter's Close, Bethnal Green E2 7AE 20, 183
St Sophia's Greek Cathedral, Moscow Road, Bayswater, W2 4LQ 87, 186
Stafford Cripps Estate, Islington, SW6 7RX 156

Stag's Head, 55 Orsman Road, N1 5RA 18, 169
Stanhope Mews South (11), Kensington, SW7 4TF 101, 102
Stanley Gardens (1), Notting Hill, W11 2ND 8, 91
Stephen Road (95), E15 3JJ 114
Stoney Street (38), Borough, SE1 9LB 42
Sumner Street, SE1 9JA 134
Surrey Quays Tube, Rotherhithe Old Road Entrance, SE16 2PP 9, 131
Sutton Court, Fauconberg Road, Chiswick W4 3JU 139
Swan Street (4), Isleworth TW7 6XA 7, 49

Talgarth Road, W14 9ES 133
Tapas Brindisa Soho, 46 Broadwick Street, W1F 7AE 161
Tate Modern, Bankside, SE1 9TG 9, 142, *143*
Tate Modern, Boiler House, East Room, Bankside, SE1 9TG 29
Tees Avenue (14), Perivale, UB6 8JH 28
Teesdale Street (88), E2 6QF 28
Teesdale Street, & Canrobert Street, E2 6PU 17
Temple Bar Memorial Dragon, WC2R 1DA 64
Temple Church, Inner Temple Lane, Temple, EC4Y 7BB 64, 99, 184
Ten Bells Pub, 84 Commercial Street, E1 6LY 9, 115, 173, *174*
Thames House, 12 Millbank, SW1P 4QE 108
Thames Path, Blackfriars Station, Southern Concourse, Hopton Street, SE1 9JH 143
The Aegean Pools, 2 Hale Lane, Mill Hill, NW7 3NX 37
The Albert, 52 Victoria Street, SW1H 0NP 140, 173
The Apple Tree, 45 Mount Pleasant, WC1X 0AE 32, 181
The Approach Tavern, 47 Approach Road, E2 9LY 166, 175
The Bacchus, 177 Hoxton Street, N1 6PJ 35, 169
The Bargehouse, Oxo Tower Wharf, Barge House Street, SE1 9PH 9, 165, *166*
The Bird in Hand, 88 Masbro Road, Brook Green W14 0LR 54, 180
The Blackfriar, 174 Queen Victoria Street, EC4V 4EG 103, 178
The Blue Posts, Berwick Street, W1F 0QA 9, 72, 179, *180*
The Builders Arms, 1 Kensington Court Place, W8 5BJ 165, 180
The Charterhouse, Charterhouse Square 9, 158
The Clapton Hart, 231 Lower Clapton Road, Lower Clapton E5 8EG 142, 145, 175
The Euro Café, 299 Caledonian Road, Islington, N1 1DT 29
The Farmiloe Building, 34-36 St John Street, EC1 4AZ 8, 105
The Grapes, 14 Lime Street, EC3M 7AN 96, 178
The Griffin, Brook Road South, Brentford, TW8 0NP 121, 181
The Griffin, Leonard Street EC2A 4RD 150, 178
The Grosvenor Pub, 76 Grosvenor Road, Pimlico, SW1V 3LA 148, 173
The Ivy House, 40 Stuart Road, Peckham, SE15 3BE 17, 172
The Joiners Arms, 116-118, Hackney Road, E2 7QL 74
The Langham Hilton, 1c Portland Place, W1B 1JA 86
The London Library, 14 St James's Square, St James's SW1Y 4LB 145
The Long Block, Gibson Gardens, Hackney N16 7HD 16
The Observatory, 64 Marchmont Street, WC1N 1AB 9, 148, *149*
The Pagoda, Pagoda gardens, Blackheath, SE3 0RE 138
The Railway Tavern Hotel, 131 Angel Lane, E15 1DB 31, 176
The Reform Club, 104 Pall Mall, SW1Y 5EW 8, 85, 88, *89*, 103, 124

The Royal Oak, 73 Columbia Road, E2 7RG 18, 20, 34, 175
The Salisbury, 1 Green Lanes, Haringey Ladder, N4 1JX 37, 169
The Shard, 32 London Bridge Street, SE1 9SG 135
The Ship & Whale, 2 Gulliver Street, SE16 7LT 9, 138, *172*, 173
The Stags Head, Orsman Road, N1 5RA 18, 169
The Standard, 10th Floor, 10 Argyle Street, WC1H 8EG 150
The Toucan, 19 Carlisle Street, W1D 3BY 9, 72, 179
The Vault, 1 Old Billingsgate Walk (Riverside, 16 Lower Thames St), EC3R 6DX
The Vaults, Leake Street, SE1 7NN 90
The Viaduct, 221 Uxbridge Road, W7 3TD 54, 180
The Waterman's Arms, 1 Glenaffric Avenue, E14 3BW 37, 176
Theed Street (2), SE1 8ST 7, 18, *19*
Thornhill Crescent, N1 1BL 118, 157
Thornley Place, SE10 9AF 33
Threadneedle Street (60), EC2R 8HP 100
Tidal Basin Road, and A1011, Silvertown Way, E16 1AD 53
Titan House, 144 Southwark Street, SE1 0UP 150
Tower Bridge, Tower Bridge Road, SE1 2UP 9, 52, 64, 145, *146*, 164
Tower of London, EC3N 4AB 8, 105, *106*, 161
Trafalgar Court, Wapping Wall, E11W 3TF 74
Trafalgar Square, WC2N 5DN 7, 40, *55*, 118
Treasury Building, Great George Street, SW1P 3JX 91
Truman Brewery, 91 Brick Lane, E1 6QR 72
Turner's Old Star, 14 Watts Street, E1W 2QG 17, 173

UK Foreign & Commonwealth Office, King Charles Street, SW1A 2AH 78
Undercroft, Lincolns Inn, Treasury Office, WC2A 3TL 78, 81, 126, 158
Underwood Street, (near Nile Street) N1 7LG 128
Unit 3, 2A Southwark Bridge Road, Bankside, SE1 9HA 24
University College, Gower Street, WC1E 6BT 63
University of the Arts, London (UAL), John Princes Street, W1G 0BJ 70
University of Westminster, Harrow Campus, Watford Road, Northwick Park Roundabout, HA1 3TP 139
Uxbridge Road (156), W12 8AA 139

Valmont Club, 266 Fulham Road, SW10 9EL 163
Vauxhall Cross (SIS Building), 85 Albert Embankment, SE11 5AW 84, 85, 86, 90
Victoria House, 37-63 Bloomsbury Square, WC1B 4DA 8, 79
Victoria Station, Terminus Place SW1V 1JR 56
Villa Road (33), Brixton, SW9 7ND 37

Walcot Stores, 68 Walcot Square, SE11 4UH 34
Wandsworth Prison, Heathfield Road, SW18 3HU 7, 46, *47*, 120
Wandsworth Youth River Club, Putney Embankment, SW15 1LS 42
Warple Way (23), Acton, W3 0RX 30
Warwick House Street (4), St James's, SW1Y 5BN 140
Water Gardens, Edgware Road, W2 2DB 88
Watergate Street, SE8 3HH 35
Waterloo Station, Eurostar Platform (Platforms 20-22), SE1 8SR 153
Waterloo Train Station, Waterloo Road, SE1 8SW 75, 78
Waterlow Park, Highgate Hill, N6 5HG 128
Waterstones, 1-3 Whittington Avenue, EC3V 1PJ 100
Weavers Field Playground, 15 Kelsey Street, E2 6HD 25
West India Quay, 26 Hertsmere Road, E14 4EG 31, 122
West Smithfield (8), EC1A 9JR 96

Westbourne Grove, W2 4UA 45
Westfield London, Ariel Way, W12 7GF 9, *152*, 153
Westminster Abbey, Broad Sanctuary, 20 Deans Yard, SW1P 3PA 8, *65*, 66
Westminster Bridge Road, SE1 7GA 8, 85
Westminster Cathedral, Victoria Street, SW1P 1LT 79
Westminster Station, SW1A 2NE 90
Westminster Underground Station, Bridge Street, SW1A 2JR 90, 162
Wheatley house 1-44 Harbridge Avenue, Roehampton SW15 4DP 56
Whipps Cross University Hospital, Whipps Cross Road, E11 1NR 162
Whitefield School, Claremont Road, Brent Cross, NW2 1AS 73
Whitehall (55), SW1A 2HP 162
Whitehall Place (1), SW1A 2HE 90, 138
Whitehall, SW1 2AY 93, 118, 78
Whitely Asset Management Ltd, 116 Princedale Road, W11 4NH 7, *56*, 57
Whitfield Street, W1T 4EU 161
Whittaker House, Richmond TW9 1EH 138
Whittlesey Street (16), Lambeth, SE1 8SZ 3, 16
Wilkes Street (4), E1 6QF 154
Wilkin Street (2), NW5 3NL 111
Wilton's Music Hall, 1 Graces Alley, Whitechapel, E1 8JB 34, 120, 126, 191
Woburn Walk, WC1H 0JL 9, 135, *136*, 156
Wood Street (74), Barbican EC2V 7WS 153
Wood Street Police Station, 37 Wood Street, Barbican, EC2P 2NQ 99
Woolwich Arsenal Station, Woolwich New Road, SE18 6EU 93
Woolwich Cemetery, Camdale Road, SE18 2DS 35, 187
Wormwood Scrubs Prison, 160 Du Cane Road, W12 0AN 8, 61, 66, 150

Ye Old Mitre Tavern, 1 Ely Court, EC1N 6SJ 9, 28, 176, 177

Areas of London (By Postcode)

N – 16, 17, 18, 20, 23, 28, 29, 30, 35, 37, 50, 52, 73, 78, 87, 103, 111, 116, 117, 118, 120, 128, 142, 147, 157, 164, 169, 170, 182, 189

NW – 30, 37, 42, 43, 44, 46, 56, 57, 58, 67, 73, 88, 100, 108, 110, 111, 118, 135, 136, 139, 140, 146, 156, 160, 161, 168, 182

E – 17, 18, 20, 21, 25, 28, 29, 30, 31, 33, 34, 36, 37, 39, 46, 49, 50, 51, 52, 53, 54, 57, 58, 62, 67, 69, 72, 73, 74, 76, 84, 101, 103, 105, 112, 114, 115, 116, 120,121,, 122, 126, 128, 134, 139, 142, 145, 151, 147, 154, 155, 159, 162, 163, 164, 166, 173, 175, 176, 182, 183, 184, 191

EC – 14, 15, 16, 20, 28, 31, 32, 40, 46, 50, 51, 53, 54, 55, m59, 64, 66, 67, 75, 76, 79, 87, 88, 88, 90, 91, 96, 99, 100, 103, 104, 105, 107, 110, 112, 114, 115, 116, 117.118, 121, 122, 123, 124, 128, 134, 139, 140, 142, 143, 145, 147, 148, 150, 151, 152, 153, 154, 155, 157, 158, 159, 160, 161, 163, 164, 165, 166, 176, 178, 184, 185

IG – 69

HA – 54, 80, 81, 84, 139

SE – 16, 17, 18, 21, 23, 24, 25, 26, 28, 29, 31, 33, 34, 35, 37, 39, 42, 52, 62, 64, 69, 75, 76, 81, 84, 85, 86, 90, 91, 93, 99, 100, 121, 100, 103, 104, 108, 110, 114, 120, 123, 124, 125, 128, 129, 131, 133, 134, 135, 138, 140, 143, 145, 150, 151, 152, 153, 156, 160, 161, 163, 165, 166, 167, 170, 171, 172, 173, 187, 189

SW – 15, 17, 2,3 24, 30, 37, 42, 46, 54, 55, 56, 57, 58, 66, 67, 70, 78, 79, 81, 83, 85, 87, 88, 90, 91, 93, 96, 99, 100, 101, 102, 103, 105 ,108, 111, 116, 118, 120,121, 122, 124, 127, 128, 129, 134, 135, 138, 139, 140, 143, 145, 146, 147, 148, 151, 156, 160, 161, 162, 163, 164, 173,187, 189, 190

TW – 34, 47, 48, 49, 121, 138, 148, 153, 158, 181, 187, 193

UB – 28, 119

W – 14, 18, 23, 24, 25, 28, 29, 30, 31, 35, 37, 39, 40, 42, 44, 45, 46, 48, 54, 56, 57, 58, 61, 64, 66, 70, 72, 73, 80, 83, 86, 87, 88, 91, 93, 94, 100, 101, 102, 103, 105, 110, 112, 117, 119, 121, 122, 123, 127, 129, 133, 135, 138, 139, 145, 146, 147, 1448, 150, 152, 156, 157, 158, 160, 161, 162, 165, 167, 178, 179, 180, 186, 192

WC –31, 32, 33, 39, 46, 55, 58, 59, 62, 63, 64, 67, 69, 73, 75, 76 78, 79, 80, 83, 86, 90, 91, 96, 101, 107, 108, 110, 111, 114, 118, 122, 124, 125, 126, 128, 134, 135, 136, 139, 142, 143, 145, 148, 150, 156, 158, 159, 160, 162, 164, 167, 181, 92